# RISK
# MANAGEMENT

## AARON LIBERMAN
### and
## MICHAEL J. WOODRUFF

FORTRESS PRESS        MINNEAPOLIS

RISK MANAGEMENT

Several sections of this book have been adapted from a book by Aaron Liberman, *A Risk and Insurance Management Guide for Medical Group Organizations*. The original book was commissioned by the Center for Research in Ambulatory Health Care Administration, a division of The Medical Group Management Association of Denver, Colorado. The authors want to express their gratitude to these organizations for their understanding and support and for permission to use and adapt the original material.

Interior design: Publishers' WorkGroup
Cover art: Kari Davis

---

**Library of Congress Cataloging-in-Publication Data**

Liberman, Aaron, 1939-
    Risk management / Aaron Liberman and Michael J. Woodruff.
    p.  cm.—(Creative pastoral care and counseling series)
    Includes bibliographical references.
    ISBN 0–8006–2758–X (alk. paper)
    1. Pastoral counseling—Law and legislation—United States.
2. Clergy—Legal status, laws, etc.—United States.  I. Woodruff,
Michael J., 1945–   .  II. Title.  III. Series.
KF4868.C44L54  1993
346.7303′3—dc20                             92–44149
[347.30633]                                 CIP

---

---

Manufactured in the U.S.A.                                 1–2758

97   96   95   94   93   1   2   3   4   5   6   7   8   9   10

# CONTENTS

90522

# PREFACE

Pastoral counseling is now a specialized practice for clergy, part of the ministry of pastoral care for thousands of clergy in diverse parish and clinical settings. It is the work of a healer who seeks to bridge two modern worlds of care: religion and medical science. The one draws upon religious insight and understanding, tradition, story, proverb, and parable. It takes theological excursions looking for a path for grace gifts to restore persons to wholeness and holiness. It depends on biblical truths, the community, and an individual sense of obligation for the care of a neighbor. It serves in order to care for souls in the old-fashioned, holistic sense of the centered identity of persons (Greek *psyche*). The other path is the way of science, although it is often called an art. Through the insights of a clinical model — an adherence to the scientific methods of observation, experimentation, description, and generalization — today's mental health care professional also seeks the healing of the mind and body. This field has appropriated the term *psyche* to identify methodologies: psychology, psychotherapy, and psychiatry.

The pastoral counselor accepts the necessity of synthesizing, of adapting in order to incorporate essential elements from both models. The healer with compassion and empathy for the wounded seeks to serve effectively and efficiently. Respecting the interrelationship and complexities of mind, body, and spirit, pastoral counselors know that effective counseling requires the discipline of study and supervised training. By these means, one can more clearly delineate ethical boundaries, clarify legal responsibilities, and develop ways to effectively deliver pastoral care. This book is about such development within the framework of a clinical practice.

We recognize that pastoral counseling is provided in multifaceted settings, often within different theological and programmatic frameworks. Both individual practitioners and counselors in pastoral counseling centers should adapt the standards described here according to their needs. Changing a practice to conform to new standards and suggestions is not easy, particularly in group settings. One goal of this book is to persuade administrators of pastoral counseling centers that it is in the best interest of the counselors and the counselees to adopt the recommended practices. We believe that a quality assurance approach to pastoral counseling requires that one adopt a programmatic approach, introducing change in incremental stages. The challenge of implementing such a program over time is not insurmountable; it is a process with several stages of development. The goal of quality assurance from a secular clinical practice perspective—as described here—complements every pastoral counselor's desire to deliver professional care competently and effectively to those in need. Pastoral counselors and their counselees will realize that a quality assurance program equips mental health care professionals to better serve their clients and thus facilitates the ministry of healing.

We also acknowledge that achieving complete agreement is impossible, even as to the terminology used to identify recipients of pastoral care. We have wrestled with this definitional challenge, and have decided to use the terms *patient*, *client*, and *counselee* interchangeably to identify the recipient of care and treatment. Customarily the term patient reflects care provided in an inpatient setting under the supervision of a physician, while client and counselee refer to persons receiving outpatient care.

We view this book as a starting point, from which readers may refine and further develop the subjects of quality assurance and practice management in pastoral counseling by using their innovativeness and considerable skills.

In writing a book for a highly specialized professional discipline such as pastoral counseling, one faces risks associated with a lack of specific knowledge about the nuances within that field. Such was the case as Aaron Liberman researched and later wrote his portion of the manuscript.

Two persons graciously contributed their time in assisting Liberman's efforts to learn more and become properly sensitive to the subject of pastoral care and counseling.

C. Roy Woodruff, Ph.D., Executive Director of the American Association of Pastoral Counselors, reviewed the initial draft of the manuscript and offered several invaluable suggestions to strengthen the text and its acceptability to its prospective readership.

Bill Hedrick, D.Min., Executive Director of Tidewater Pastoral Counseling Services, recognized a significant gap in Liberman's understanding of the role of the confessional quality of confidence and its pervasive influence upon the care/cure process. In his typically diplomatic manner, Dr. Hedrick provided proper guidance and some good old-fashioned sensitivity training.

# INTRODUCTION: PASTORAL CARE AND PROFESSIONAL LIABILITY

Because of a growing sense of risk and exposure to litigation, obtaining adequate professional liability insurance has become a genuine concern of pastoral counselors and others providing human services. The issue is professional liability; the concern is the ever-increasing number of liability claims among those providing human services. A professional's future portends both uncertainty and unknown costs when the normative expectation of maintaining one's practice is that litigation is inevitable. An abiding concern driving this issue to a heightened level of discussion is that professional liability insurance for years has fluctuated in cost; and, in some instances, its pricing has been a victim of factors affecting the availability of insurance for specific groups of professionals. At one time, the issue of professional liability coverage for health service providers affected only persons with medical degrees. Nonmedical providers were thought to be accountable to medical professionals and were not considered as independent agents for whom insurance was necessary and appropriate.

For years, the cost of professional liability insurance has been a function of economic factors affecting the insurance marketplace in general. During periods of change, a lack of market competition often severely compromised the cost of maintaining coverage for specific groups of professionals. For example, during the 1980s a crisis of confidence reduced the availability of professional liability insurance and the willingness and capability of insurance carriers to maintain a stream of coverage for human services providers. At issue was both the availability of insurance and the insurability of various professional service providers. This issue became a particular concern as human service professionals tried to defend themselves amid allegations and claims of professional incompetence, misconduct, or mismanagement. Litigation requires descriptions and explanations of a professional's conduct. Without documentation to support the rationale of a particular course of treatment, a health care provider has no viable means of defense. This vulnerability puts insurance carriers in an untenable position, which is reflected in either an unwillingness to cover a class of risk or an inflated premium structure.

This problem persisted throughout the 1980s, and an editorial appearing in *Best's Review* (May 1991, 47) indicated that people are more likely to sue medical providers now than they were in the past. For that article a Gallup poll of one thousand health care consumers showed that 47 percent agreed with this statement.

If one expands the notion of litigation to include nonmedical health care providers, the question becomes why individuals are more likely to pursue litigation against a provider today than in years past. Although people expect professional compliance, they will generally sue only when they believe they will succeed. Without records both private practitioners and those associated with human services organizations are ill equipped to provide a credible defense in the event something goes awry in the provider-patient relationship.

Not all professional provider-patient relationships will terminate harmoniously. Hence it is essential that therapists maintain documents to attest to and defend their approach to treatment. Such a practice should become a standard and integral procedure in therapeutic care.

The human services professions present a classic study of both medicoprofessional and psychological interaction and the establishment of socioprofessional relationships predicated on trust. The fabric of this unique blend of disciplines encourages a basic assumption that the service being purchased (health care) answers a need both for treatment and the correction of an existing abnormality of either a personality dysfunction or a personal relationship. As the relationship between provider and patient develops over time, ample evidence suggests that the patient makes more assumptions and becomes more trusting—often without a discernible rationale. Thus the patient tends to depend more on the knowledge and goodwill of the provider. When patient and provider disagree about care or method, the conflict more often than not resembles the breakup of a friendship, with all the emotion such a rupture can engender.

One can often attribute such problems to a breakdown in communication or an unwillingness to meet the other's expectation. The patient's heightened sense of loss, disappointment, and even anguish can further aggravate this situation. There also appears to be a pattern of frustration on the part of the provider. The result is frequently the termination of the relationship.

This scenario is common in the human services field. One of the more frustrating aspects of the breakup relates to situations that may arise later on when the patient seeks redress for a grievance. At this time the patient challenges the ability of the provider to make a justifiable defense. Without a documented means to accomplish that defense, the provider often cannot justify the rationale for the care. In such instances, the presence of an active treatment plan accompanied by progress notes becomes a necessity. This is true for all providers who participate in the care and treatment of patients.

## PASTORAL COUNSELORS AND PASTORS

At this point, it is important to identify and to distinguish between pastors, pastoral counselors, and human services providers. For purposes of this text, the term *human services provider* refers to any person designated to provide a counseling or psychotherapeutic service by nature of that person's degree, licensure, or appointment status. The term *pastoral counselor* refers to a person holding a pastoral degree or designation who is appointed or hired to provide professional counseling or psychotherapeutic services to an individual or to a group of patients.

The highly publicized California clergy malpractice case *Nally v. Grace Community Church* (253 Cal. Rptr. 1988, 97) distinguished between parish pastors, providing free counseling, and pastoral counselors. The parish pastors were held to the same standards of negligence as other people; the pastor's activity did not create a higher standard. But a footnote in the opinion said that pastoral counselors who charge a fee and hold themselves out as mental health care providers may create a special relationship and a higher standard of care. The California Supreme Court faced the definitional question and opted for a pastoral model, not a medical one, in characterizing what parish clergy did when they counseled. Under the pastoral model, the legal implication seems both pejorative—parish pastors do not provide a professional service when they counsel—and commendatory—pastoral counselors, particularly those functioning in clinical settings, are professionals because their role fits within a medical model.

Although legally important, the distinction does not matter for our purpose, which is to address the situation of pastoral counselors who provide mental health care services and accept a medical model, probably utilizing psychotherapeutic theory and techniques, as a primary source for delivering quality pastoral care. First, any clergy engaged in a counseling activity (whether under a pastoral care model or a medical model) need professional liability insurance to provide a legal defense against unjustified claims. Second, when defending against a lawsuit, clergy will be asked during their deposition for explanations of their counseling, including observations, concerns, advice, recommendations, and referrals. If they produce no notes or records or invoke a confidentiality privilege, they risk making little or no defense and having the plaintiff's case unopposed.

Numerous pastors and pastoral counselors want their counsel to be absolutely insulated from litigation. They conduct their pastoral counseling in highly confidential settings. To reduce the risk of later discovery or of review by third parties they take no notes. They even resist disclosure of the counselee's identity as within the scope of their confidential privilege. These counselors do well not to think of their work within a medical model. They are confessors who guard secrets appropriately and legally. Accordingly, they should stay within character, maintaining careful boundaries and making referrals to pastoral counselors, who integrate insights from both theological and psychological training.

Because pastoral counseling is a professional activity that virtually any member of the clergy can be called upon to provide, we address this book and its suggestions to all clergy who provide professional counseling services. When litigation occurs, the plaintiff does not distinguish those who have received the sanctioned designation of an accrediting body from those who have not. Rather, the plaintiff and attorney would likely focus on and address the alleged wrongful act and its alleged perpetrator.

Our goal is to encourage any person providing a pastoral counseling service to practice with the potential need for a legal defense always in mind. All human services providers should also adhere to this principle of practice management.

### Trust as a Sole Means of Defense

Human services providers, particularly mental health clinicians, are influential fiduciaries of power. They are skilled in the art of persuasion, which is one of the means whereby clinicians effect changes in clients' behaviors or performances. Patients are frequently anxious to the point of impaired judgment in wishing to satisfy the expectations of their therapist. With the desire to please, patients accept suggestions and self-persuasion occurs; patients may precipitously accept any thought to satisfy an immediate need at the expense of their long-term welfare.

When patients subordinate their treatment objective to satisfy the clinician, the implications of that decision become even more pronounced. In this sphere of influence health care providers must exert caution and not even seem to attempt to coerce patients into a situation that one could construe as compromising either the welfare of patients or the credibility of therapists.

### Money in the Therapeutic Relationship

Money plays a role in determining from whom a consumer will purchase a therapeutic service. Pastoral counselors who charge a fee for services implicitly offer counselees a therapeutic service. The medical model then attaches to the providers (Hedrick 1992). Once pastoral counselors charge money for services provided, they lose legal immunity. If the patient knows and likes the pastoral counselor, the patient may well ignore common sense and rely on unprofessional advice because of a belief that the pastoral counselor, a friend and a professional, would not lead her or him astray.

How often have patients entered an initial therapy session thinking how unenthused they are about the encounter? Yet when such patients emerge from the session, they feel refreshed and positive about the therapist. All therapists have probably experienced this phenomenon within their own practice.

Patients might infer that because they view the seller (therapist) as competent or adept at what they do, therefore the product the therapist represents (mental health care) must be equally good. This adulation of and respect for the therapist both strengthens the relationship and potentially compromises the future success of therapy and the therapeutic relationship, because as the excessive confidence of patients is manifested, so too are their expectations heightened, often to a point of unreality. This situation poses a challenge to the therapist. Indeed, the need to engender a feeling of confidence in the patient represents a major function of the role and responsibility of the therapist as a health care provider. Nonetheless, the therapist must at the same time maintain a realistic perspective regarding the outcomes that can be achieved during treatment. It is incumbent upon the therapist to have in place necessary defenses in the form of process notes and documentation in the event a professional relationship goes awry.

## A PLAN FOR
## MAINTAINING PROFESSIONAL RELATIONS

The ability of a therapist to manage a relationship in large part depends on the ongoing management of the professional relationship itself. In accomplishing this end, the therapist must maintain systems and records that provide an appropriate audit trail of the patient's progress and the rationale for the treatment being employed. This book has as its objective to present a plan for maintaining ongoing professional relationships that are backed and supported by an audit process and documentation which enhances the defensibility of the treatment administered to a patient. The approach employed here includes a definition of the responsibilities of the therapist and a presentation of recommended methods of implementing, maintaining, and documenting the fulfillment of those responsibilities.

This book applies both to individual private practice providers and to those affiliated with group practices, proprietorships, and corporate organizations. Several areas of concern are addressed. An outline of objectives is presented narratively as standards of practice; each objective includes a discussion of the methods of compliance that one can employ in maintaining the quality of clinical practice. The first segment of the discussion addresses the issue of quality assurance. The premise is that each practitioner should maintain an ongoing and documentable quality assurance mechanism, which is designed objectively to monitor the quality of practice and to evaluate the appropriateness of the care being provided.

The second area of concern relates to the maintenance of clinical records and the elements of information that should be documented within the clinical records system.

The third area of concern relates to the practitioner's responsibility in addressing the rights of clients, in developing an ability to address objectively grievances of clients, and in providing redress in the event a grievance is proved correct. This segment includes the process for receiving and handling any grievances or claims that are filed against either an individual or a provider organization.

The fourth segment relates to the referral of patients to other counselors who may be able to provide more appropriate care in addressing the patient's immediate needs.

The fifth area is that of practice management resources, which includes information that one can use to establish systems and procedures for the maintenance of a quality private practice and a sound health care organization including the purchase of proper insurance coverages to protect against liability exposures.

Although the management of a practice and the success in maintaining patient relationships rest ultimately with the counselor or therapist, the development of a quality assurance mechanism facilitates a relationship in which the client's needs are both respected and addressed, even when the level of the relationship does not meet the ongoing expectations of the client or the provider. Only within this framework can one satisfy and utilize the client's future needs and expectations to enhance the potential for an ultimate recovery.

In essence, this book establishes a basis for all counselors to become the risk managers of their own individual practices or for the risk management resources that they can develop to a positive extent within a corporate setting or a group practice.

# 1

# ESTABLISHING STANDARDS FOR QUALITY ASSURANCE

Since the 1980s, legal liability exposures of all health and human services providers have expanded alarmingly. The landmark case that opened the doors to litigation was *Darling v. Charleston Community Hospital*, which was decided in Illinois in 1965. The court granted payment of $110,000 in damages to a patient due to the negligence of hospital emergency room staff. The physician involved in the case admitted his liability, thereby leaving the path clear for an abrogation of the doctrine of charitable immunity as it pertained to hospital settings. Although the circumstances surrounding the Darling case would be cumbersome to explain, the following remarks made for the record in the court proceedings that cited the Darling case are helpful:

> The conception that the hospital does not undertake to treat the patient, does not undertake to act through its doctors and nurses, but undertakes instead simply to procure them to act upon their own responsibility, no longer reflects the fact. Present day hospitals, as their manner of operation plainly demonstrates, do far more than furnish facilities for treatment. They regularly employ on a salary basis a large staff of physicians, nurses, and interns, as well as administrative and manual workers, and they charge patients for medical care and treatment, collecting for such services, if necessary, by legal action. Certainly, the person who avails himself of hospital facilities expects that the hospital will attempt to cure him, not that its nurses or other employees will act on their own responsibility. (George 1970, 26–27)

The decisions following *Darling* not only removed charitable immunity as a means of exploration but also placed more responsibility on trustee boards, directors of organizations, and associated staff to assure that the quality of care satisfies some basic standards (George 1970, 26–27). In addition, they strongly suggest that the staff obey the rules and regulations of an organization and that those empowered with the responsibilities for care and treatment adhere to appropriate methods of analysis, referral, and follow-up. Pastoral counselors may invoke different precedents relative to the treatment of their clients; nonetheless the imprint and expectations generated from the

13

post-*Darling* decisions reflect on the present-day expectations of those involved in pastoral care.

This chapter is primarily designed to provide a listing of suggested expectations for those involved in pastoral care and counseling; implicit within the positive recommendations are a number of negative recommendations that those providing care and treatment should consider. The program set forth is designed to monitor, evaluate, and improve on the quality and appropriateness of ongoing care. The method here is to present a standard and, where necessary, an explanation of the method(s) of compliance that one should follow when properly establishing a quality assurance program for those in the pastoral counseling professions.

## STANDARD 1

Each pastoral counseling practice or organization should have an ongoing quality assurance program (QA) designed to monitor, evaluate, and improve on the quality and appropriateness of the pastoral care being provided.

### Methods of Compliance

a. Review annually and monitor clinical practices
b. Review annually and evaluate clinical service policies
c. Modify clinical service policies as needed

The thesis of this standard is that the pastoral counseling organization (PCO) should require the establishment and ongoing maintenance of an effective QA program. The program should be supported by a process that has as its basis the following activities established at regular intervals: the review and monitoring of clinical practices; and the review, evaluation, and modification of clinical service policies at least annually.

In addition, individual practices, corporate organizations, and group practices should have a written and formalized plan for the QA program that describes in concise terms the mechanisms being implemented to maintain the effectiveness of the program. Also, the scope of the QA program should include at least the following activities:

1. The quality and appropriateness of diagnostic procedures
2. The quality and appropriateness of ongoing treatment procedures
3. The completeness of clinical record entries
4. The actual performance of administering pastoral care
5. The evaluation of patient satisfaction
6. The quality and appropriateness of intervention and referral mechanisms for emergency treatment

## STANDARD 2

One should have an ongoing method for the collection and review of information about significant aspects of pastoral care for each client.

### Methods of Compliance
a. Clear statement of the purpose of care for each client
b. Profile of significant characteristics requiring modification for each client
c. Maintenance of standard information checklist for all clients seen in therapy
d. Name of referral source used when deemed appropriate

The methods of evaluation to determine the level of compliance with this standard should include the identification of preferred clinical approaches to improve care and the identification of problems that may impede that possibility. The information collection and the evaluation processes working in tandem afford an opportunity to identify areas of concern that can result in problems for the counselee or family. This standard should also provide a mechanism whereby the counselor can refer a client to another provider when he or she is unable to address either the immediate or the long-term requirements of a specific situation.

## STANDARD 3

One should have a written protocol with appropriate and documented expectations for the improvement of clinical care once one has identified problems.

### Methods of Compliance
a. Involvement of colleagues
b. Presentation of clearly defined objectives

An individual practitioner or even a group of practitioners should not develop a written protocol in isolation. In establishing a written protocol with the attendant requirements for documentation it seems both necessary and appropriate to involve other professionals within the field who are not directly related to or the beneficiaries of the practice being addressed.

## STANDARD 4

One should have documented clinical oversight to assure that improvements in the quality of patient care are initiated.

*Methods of Compliance*

a. Patient care committee or peer review
b. Status of problems identified and followed
c. Communication between reviewer and counselor
d. Scope and effectiveness of QA assessed annually
e. Inadequacies corrected

A pastoral counseling center can address compliance with this standard through the establishment of a patient care committee, which provides on-going oversight on behalf of all counselors associated with the organization. For the pastoral counselor in an individual practice, this standard provides a challenge, but one must address it in order to establish a documented QA oversight process. One can accomplish this standard by using one's peers as reviewers of the treatment that an individual counselor prescribes. Within a community that has several counselors available, peer review committees could and should be established to effect that care and treatment. In small communities with few counselors, the pastoral counselors would have the responsibility to ask their national association to help provide an ongoing mechanism of review and oversight.

Whether one refers to an individual practice, a group practice, or a corporate practice, one should address at least three methods of compliance:

1. One should recognize and follow the status of identified problems to assure improvement or resolution
2. The reviewer and the counselor should communicate necessary information when problems arise or opportunities to improve the delivery of care involve more than a single treatment modality
3. One should review and assess at least annually the scope and the effectiveness of a QA program

Once accomplished, this procedure provides a mechanism whereby one can correct inadequacies in the system and establish monitoring techniques to assure that the program operates properly.

## STANDARD 5

The PCO should deliver services that demonstrate high-quality patient care. The services should be provided in a manner consistent with the principles of professional practice established by the provider's organization and national society, and should reflect ongoing concern for the acceptability, accessibility, and availability of these services.

*Methods of Compliance*
a. Consistent with principles of professional practice
b. Reflect concern for acceptability, accessibility and availability of services
c. Description of system for providing services
d. Standard Operating Procedure (SOP) available for referral in an emergency
e. SOP for informing client of persons providing care
f. Demonstration of use of all diagnostic procedures
g. Documentation of availability of consultation
h. Assure that all clinical information is made part of permanent clinical record

In complying with this standard, one should describe the general system for providing patient services both during and after normal hours of operation. It is essential that each pastoral counselor have a SOP for referring patients to necessary medical or psychiatric resources in the event of an emergency that is beyond the counselor's capability.

One should provide emergency care information to all clients when they enter treatment.

Have in place a mechanism of informing clients of the names, professions, and titles of all professionals providing for their care. Providers and their organizations often take this part of the process for granted. They sometimes assume that patients know the professional credentials of their providers. When patients do not know, they can become uneasy and, in extreme unattended cases, go to litigation because they construe that they have been misinformed or ill-advised about the treatment being provided.

One should document the use of acceptable diagnostic procedures, including—but not necessarily limited to—referral for medical services that may become necessary. The clinical record should note when a physician, psychologist, or other professional has been called into a case for consultation; and, wherever possible, the observations of the evaluating physician should be documented as an anecdotal note in the record of the referring pastoral counselor.

Also document the availability and use of acceptable consultation, when such is necessary. As mentioned, the use of medical or other professional consultation certainly merits a note in the clinical record of the patient who is referred for care.

All mechanisms of compliance with the standard regarding the delivery of clinical services should become a permanent part of each patient's record when clinically appropriate and important to the treatment process.

## STANDARD 6

One should provide written documentation and other appropriate evidence of the continuity of patient care.

### Methods of Compliance

a. Evidence of timely follow-up
b. Consistent use of treatment plan
c. Consistent use of patient consent form
d. Consistent use of problem list

Compliance with this standard should include reasonable follow-up regarding patient adherence to the proposed plan of care. This standard presumes that the counselor provides a plan of care at least during the client's second visit. Once the counselor provides and adopts a plan of care, one should require the client to sign an acknowledgment form that this care is being provided and has been accepted as an appropriate mode of treatment. This form provides both informed consent for the client and an excellent method of documentation in the event a disillusioned or angry client files a claim at a later date. In addition, this form affords an audit trail for the counselor in order to assure that the records are appropriately monitored and evaluated for compliance with the initial treatment plan.

For clients who are either incapable of understanding the information provided or are not physically or mentally competent to have the information presented to them, one should present this material to a parent or guardian who is able to understand the implications of the clinical decisions that have gone into the establishment of the treatment plan.

## STANDARD 7

One should demonstrate concern for minimizing the cost of care to all clients.

### Methods of Compliance

a. Studies of treatment relevance
b. Studies of treatment timeliness
c. Studies of treatment effectiveness
d. Studies of duplication of services provided
e. Studies of cost effectiveness

To comply with this standard, a reviewer(s) unrelated to the clinical practice being evaluated should study the relevance of treatment services. The system of review should include a utilization review component in which the reviewer evaluates the documents of the clinical record and assesses the time-liness and appropriateness of services.

One should also have QA evaluations that review the cost-effectiveness of the diagnostic and treatment services for specific categories. When one iden-tifies an untimely or inappropriate use of services, or recognizes new clinical needs of the client, one should have procedures in place for instituting cor-rective action.

It is axiomatic that the counselor should not duplicate or have unnecessary diagnostic or ongoing treatment procedures. Rather, through case manage-ment and individualized treatment plans one can assure the appropriate use of services. A treatment plan should encompass all aspects of the services being provided.

Pastoral counseling centers may have the resources to assess the cost-ben-efit factors of the services they have provided to their clients. Such studies can not only provide an effective QA mechanism but also serve as an excellent marketing resource. The prudent use of the dollar is an issue that will not soon retire, and it represents an everyday concern of virtually all persons. Therefore an evaluation and objective assessment of the cost-effectiveness of services can afford both active and prospective clients an excellent perspective on their treatment and the handling of their care by the therapist.

## STANDARD 8

One should have quarterly QA meetings that afford those persons partic-ipating in the QA process an opportunity both to comment on one an-other's activities and to share insights as to appropriate mechanisms for improving the quality of practice of each participant.

### Methods of Compliance

a. Evidence of sharing of views
b. Minutes documenting each meeting held
c. Evidence of efforts to correct improper treatment techniques
d. Evidence of persistent efforts to improve quality of care provided

The Japanese have for years used a concept of quality circles as a means of involving employees in the development of better manufacturing and overall business practices. Here management and line staff together troubleshoot problems, whether they are manufacturing challenges or labor-management issues, and work out consensual solutions. One can extend this concept to clinical practice, where all practitioners have a similar vested interest in assur-ing that they make available a quality product to their patients. Through the use of the quality circle concept, counselors can achieve this objective and assure clients that they will receive the best care from knowledgeable professionals, who in turn assist one another in improving their treatment technology.

Peter Senge advocates a discipline or concept he calls team learning, which is useful for all pastoral counseling centers: "Unless teams can learn, the organization cannot learn." According to Senge "discipline" is a "body of theory and technique that must be studied and mastered to be put into practice. A discipline is a developmental path for acquiring certain skills or competencies. . . . Thus, a corporation cannot be 'excellent' in the sense of having arrived at a permanent excellence; it is always in the state of practicing the disciplines of learning, of becoming better or worse." Team learning is vital to QA of any organization (Senge 1990, 424).

For individual practitioners, the use of a QA program that involves one's colleagues in the evaluation process may prove to be a significant advantage in both reducing the chronicity of problems that may occur during treatment and in enhancing the ability of the counselor to provide top-quality care to all clients.

By implementing a QA process that includes the previously noted mechanisms for evaluation, both private practitioners and organizational-based pastoral care providers establish a mechanism of accountability that can not only serve the ongoing needs of clients but also provide a method of protecting both the integrity of a clinical practice and the accountability of its adherents.

# 2

---

# MAINTAINING
# CLINICAL RECORDS

Clinical records provide a documented source of information as well as a chronology of significant and routine events during a client's counseling program. The information contained in a clinical record is invaluable in establishing the basis for either continuing or terminating counseling and in assessing the success of treatment in terms of outcomes (changes of behavior or attitudes) achieved during the course of counseling. Some may believe that less documentation of clinical impressions results in reduced exposure to a successful liability claim. Ordinarily, however, nothing could be further from the truth. Liability exposures are a hazard of any professional counseling practice that charges fees or uses psychological techniques. Proper documentation of client care provides an objective record for justifying the advice given and any actions taken.

## THE FIVE ASPECTS OF AN
## INFORMATION SYSTEM

There are five primary parts to establishing and maintaining a complete, ongoing clinical record system.

### Establishing the Information System

This phase of establishing an information system sets goals, standards, and parameters for the collection and retention of information. Who collects the information? What standard information should be taken? Should printed forms be used? How should dates be stored? What type of filing system is needed? During this phase one makes initial decisions about the kind of system one will employ.

### Collecting the Data

Information collected during the intake interviews and in the course of counseling should be in the form of both factual and anecdotal data provided by both the counselor and the client. This information should include vital historical data about the client as well as contemporary data that provide a clinical biography of the client and describe the counseling history, which is essential to establishing a counseling plan. The focus is on acquiring relevant information.

## Maintaining the Record

The maintenance of information regarding a client provides for the standardization of an information system so that from one patient to the next the same format is followed, thus affording a sense of organization to the clinical records system.

## Storing the Record

This phase establishes a standard of maintaining a record of both the number of years that record will be stored and the method by which the record will be stored.

## Retrieving Information

This phase provides for various mechanisms whereby the counselor accesses the system of information storage for information needed to continue treatment.

## THREE CONSIDERATIONS

### Isolating Pertinent Information

Each clinical records system should have a mechanism whereby specific information pertinent to a client enables the counselor to provide immediate care. This feature again points to the importance of having a standardized system of information entry within a clinical record in order to assure that a counselor can readily obtain information needed for a client's care.

One format in developing a clinical record is to split the record into two parts, each having a divider. The left half of the record is for nonclinical information and for a problem list that summarizes pertinent issues and problems identified during the course of counseling. The right half of the record contains all the clinical information and includes the following sections:

1. Client information section, consisting of a face sheet containing biographical information about the patient, a registration form, and consent forms
2. Correspondence section, containing items like release forms, insurance or disability forms, letters mailed to the client, a treatment authorization request form, and miscellaneous information
3. Clinical notes section, containing copies of clinical notes that the counse-

lor provides after each session (later this chapter discusses more about clinical or progress notes entered into the clinical record).

One must also protect clinical records from loss, alteration, and destruction. This element includes the development of a policy regarding the storage of records so that the information on each client is available at all times. At times a third party who is involved either in the financing of care or in the actual provision of services requires information on a client. It is essential that one have a system of checkout so that when records are loaned to specific authorized individuals who are associated with the treatment program (e.g., a supervisor previously authorized by a client to review the record), the counselor, records administrator, or secretary has an audit trail to the location of that record. Using a checkout procedure of following records authorized for use by third parties provides the most ready means of accountability as to the location of a given record at any time during the treatment program.

## Protecting Confidentiality

The clinical records pertaining to an individual client are the property of the counselor or the organization for which that counselor works. Each clinical record must be maintained to serve the client, the provider, and the organization in accordance with established legal and clinical requirements. The information contained in the record is the property of the client, and the client is entitled to protection of that information. Consequently, the provider and organization are professionally and morally obligated not to use the content of the clinical record in any manner that would jeopardize the client's interest. The only exception is that the organization may use the record if necessary to defend itself. The purposes for which information is used may be classified as follows:

1. As a method of communication among and between the attending counselors during the current process of treatment
2. As a reference for treatment of future conditions attendant to the specific client involved
3. For training personnel and for assisting counselors-in-training and students to relate theory to practice
4. For evaluation of the quality of care through a review and analysis of patterns of care as documented in the clinical record
5. For the promotion of effective and efficient use of facilities, equipment, services, personnel, and financial resources through employment of statistical analyses abstracted from the record
6. For research aimed at the improvement of treatment and the assessment of appropriate cases to determine methods of diagnosis
7. For documentation that demonstrates conformity to government regulations

8. For follow-up care of clients with chronic conditions and for the assessment of services rendered

One can and should disclose information in the clinical record to professionals in order to aid them in conducting peer review on the quality of care
or in assessing the competence or qualification of an individual counselor. In
such cases the reviewing parties should sign acknowledgments and commit-
ments that they will not use the information contained in the clinical record
for any personal gain but only in fulfilling their peer review responsibilities.

### Designating Person to Maintain Records

A multiclinician pastoral counseling center should designate a specific person
or office to handle all clinical records and information attendant to each client
record. In an individual practice either the counselor or a secretary must be
responsible for maintaining the content and the quality of the clinical record.
The designated person assumes a major obligation of trust. Within this setting, there is a risk that the information and communication system will break
down. This breakdown could ultimately lead to the loss of quality control in
the handling of client records, and would affect the quality of pastoral care.

## DATA COLLECTION POLICY

Any persons involved in the collection, handling, or dissemination of client
information should be specifically informed of their responsibility to protect
the information under their control and of the substantial penalties that may
accrue if they violate the trust inherent in the handling of information.

In an employer-employee situation, the proven violation of confidentiality
of information is grounds for at least immediate termination of access to further data, if not for immediate discharge. One should inform all employees of
this policy at the time of employment or upon adoption of a confidentiality
policy. The employee should sign an acknowledgment form, which should be
maintained in the employee's personnel record. Even in a private practice
with a solo practitioner and perhaps only a secretary, the practitioner should
advise the secretary in writing that the secretary is responsible for maintaining confidentiality. The practitioner should also require the secretary to sign
an acknowledgment form that spells out the severe penalties if he or she ab-
rogates the policy in any manner.

Clients should be granted access to the content of their counseling record
at all times. If a client wishes to correct or amend information in the record,
one should handle such a change as an amendment, acknowledging the client's request; one should not change the original record entry. Furthermore,
one should identify this information as an additional document appended to

the record at the client's direction. Once inserted, the information should be considered an integral part of the clinical record.

The subject of appropriate record keeping deserves a special comment for clients who avail themselves of pastoral counseling service as a form of treatment for a mental health care problem, or for a family or marital crisis, rather than as a means of satisfying a confessional. First, from the perspective of the medical model, one records a client's history, the client's complaints and concerns, observations, and the course of pastoral counseling given. This clinical record is not taking notes, a practice of many counselors. The distinction is critical. A journal that a counselor keeps for research notes, reading sources, and ideas to explore is not part of the client file. The informal, personal journal notes of the pastoral counselor that do not refer to client names should not substitute for the discipline and art of maintaining an appropriate clinical record for each client seen.

To keep a second set of counseling records to maintain client secrets in absolute confidentiality is unnecessary and impractical: the judicial penalty for nondisclosure of such a record upon receipt of a subpoena duces tecum for all records could be severe.

The counselor sometimes talks with a client's family member about the counselee's problems. The counselor should keep the information received confidential, particularly when opinions and other facts would be adverse to the counselee. One may open a separate, but cross-indexed, information file, thereby averting a risk of discovery by the counselee. If the material were otherwise placed in the client's clinical file and the client discovered it, not only might it adversely affect the client emotionally, but, without a waiver from the family member, the counselor would be committing a separate breach of confidentiality.

The remainder of this chapter deals with recommended standards for the establishment of a quality clinical records system.

## STANDARD 9

The PCO should maintain a clinical records system that provides accurately documented information regarding the ongoing treatment and progress of clients.

### *Methods of Compliance*

a. Standardized records format for all counselees
b. Parameters set for information collection and retention
c. Standardized procedures for information retrieval
d. System to protect clinical records from loss, alteration, or destruction
e. Designation of staff member to maintain and secure records
f. Standard data collection and retention policy

## STANDARD 10

After each session the counselor should make notes and enter the document into the clinical records system, which should be readily accessible to the practitioner(s) involved in the treatment and care of that client.

### Methods of Compliance

  a. Treatment progress duly noted
  b. Timely updating of records
  c. Attending clinician signs and dates entry
  d. When deemed appropriate, note entry on problem list

A counselor who fails to document properly and punctually each client encounter exposes the practice or organization to unnecessary hardship if a claim is filed. One of the reasons for the term *clinical hour* is to reflect the fact that ten to fifteen minutes of that hour are set aside for the therapist to make notations relating to that visit.

The performance evaluation of each therapist should take into account the quality of clinical records support and documentation that the respective therapists provide.

Some pastoral counseling organizations have established contractual relationships with their clinicians in order to formalize the expectations of each party and to eliminate future misunderstanding and minimize the chances of professional conflict. Such contractual relationships should include a binding requirement for proper support for all policies governing clinical record maintenance as a condition of continuing employment.

## STANDARD 11

The clinical records system should be standardized to the extent that the general format of each clinical record contains essentially the same components of information and provides access to that information for contemplation and follow-up.

### Methods of Compliance

  a. Should contain client biographical information
  b. Should contain registration form
  c. Should contain consent form
  d. Should contain release of information form
  e. Should contain a diagnosis
  f. Should contain an ongoing problem list
  g. Should contain a progress notes section
  h. Should contain consultant reports
  i. Should contain medical examination report

The methods of compliance to achieve the clinical records standards include the following:

1. The PCO should develop and maintain an ongoing documented system for the collection, processing, maintenance, storage, and retrieval of clinical record information
2. Clinical information referring to a particular client should be readily available to the practitioner providing care
3. The clinical record should be protected from loss, tampering, alteration, destruction, or unauthorized disclosure of information
4. A designated staff person should be in charge of the maintenance and quality of all clinical records
5. One should have written policies concerning clinical records that should include:
   a. Entry of date of service into the clinical records
   b. Maintenance of confidentiality of information
   c. Mechanisms to safeguard clinical records from loss
   d. Release of information contained in the clinical records
   e. Requirement concerning consent of a guardian to counseling of a minor or an incompetent
   f. Retention of active clinical records
   g. Retirement and storage of inactive clinical records

## STANDARD 12

One should have a written policy statement requiring a standard format of information contained in the clinical record.

### Methods of Compliance

a. Policy statement should be clearly stated and unequivocal
b. Policy statement should require consistent format in all clinical records
c. Policy statement should present implications of not following requirements of stated policy for clinician use of clinical records

The standardization requirement has nine components for the format of and information contained in the clinical record for each counseling session. The basic data (source of referral; mental health history, including hospitalizations; name of family or personal physician; address; and telephone number) will already have been collected and made part of the file. The nine components are:

1. Date of treatment
2. Name and profession of the practitioner providing the treatment

3. Primary complaint or purpose of the visit
4. Clinical findings during the visit
5. Clinical diagnosis
6. Counseling provided
7. Disposition, recommendations, and instructions to the client
8. Signature or initials of the practitioner providing treatment
9. Referral practitioners recommended to the client and the name of the counselor whom the client has visited

## STANDARD 13

All clinical reports within the record should be considered a permanent part of the clinical record.

### Methods of Compliance

a. Retain for at least 7 years
b. Until information is disposed of, should be treated as confidential
c. Use filing system for inactive clients which is consistent with system employed for active clients

To comply with this standard, one should consider information like progress notes, other diagnostic impressions, and reports from external consultants, as well as any notations made by the client, to be an integral and permanent part of the clinical record. As such, these items should be protected from loss, alteration, or destruction. It is essential that one retain the counselor's progress notes in an unaltered and permanent state. One should complete any alterations made to the notes, with the date of alteration as well as any other relevant information noted in the chart.

## STANDARD 14

The PCO should establish a clinical records review process.

### Methods of Compliance

a. Should include a utilization review process
b. Should include a client services review process
c. Should include a clinical records review process
d. Should include a staff development program (continuing education for private practitioner)
e. Should include a patient rights program

The primary purposes of the clinical records review process are to develop and maintain a unified and consistent records maintenance system and to develop control mechanisms for the revision and updating of clinical records. Chapter 3 addresses recommendations for the establishment of a clinical records review process, and this standard is discussed there.

In developing a clinical records system for an individual private practice or a pastoral counseling organization, one must be trained and instructed as to the expectations of the system. The maintenance of a uniform system of clinical records is difficult for the individual practitioner because the routine requirements involved often detract or take time from a clinical practice. Therefore, as previously noted in the discussion of the quality assurance program, it becomes increasingly important for clinical practitioners to have the opportunity to interact with one another in a formal setting, to discuss methods, and to effect procedures that establish the proper maintenance of clinical records.

# 3

# CONDUCTING RECORDS REVIEW

Once a viable clinical records management system has been established, an ongoing clinical services and records review system is needed. The components of such a viable system should consist of the following functional areas of responsibility:

1. Utilization review process
2. Client services review process
3. Clinical records review process
4. Staff development process
5. Patient rights process

The utilization review process evaluates the timeliness of treatment and the necessity of the care being provided. The purpose of utilization review is to identify those instances in which a counselor may be under- or overtreating a client and to recommend corrective measures to maintain the treatment plan at a realistic level.

The client services review process evaluates the actual provision of care and the content of treatment as it relates to the client's problem(s). This process normally detects deficiencies in the treatment that might lead to a deterioration of the mental, emotional, or physical state of a client.

The clinical records review process evaluates the content of clinical records in relation to the services being provided. The responsibility of this process is to determine whether the client record provides information that accurately reflects the type of treatment being provided and to eliminate future inconsistencies in clinical information entries included as part of a client's permanent record.

The staff development process monitors the opportunities for employees to attend professional development seminars. It also establishes a pattern of practice that enhances staff ability to perform and respond properly to the treatment needs of clients.

The patient rights process normally concerns client rights, any grievances emanating from the treatment of a client or family, and the means employed to resolve disputes that arise.

Compared to a solo practitioner, a pastoral counseling center with multiple employees can more easily establish a comprehensive clinical services and records review system, because each practitioner in the center can play an integral role in the process through single or multiple committee appointments. In such a setting, counselors usually convene on a monthly basis. If a governing board oversees the center, the center submits a quarterly report to the governance authority regarding the activities of the committees and any significant exceptions that have been noted and corrected as a result of the committee process.

For individual practitioners, the task is more challenging in that the individual practitioner does not have significant time available to manage such a program. Nonetheless, one can establish this process on a cooperative basis with other solo practitioners. Using such a system, the practitioners can convene on a regular basis to review their respective caseloads. Thus they can achieve the same positive outcomes as centers with multiple employees.

Whether an individual practitioner, a group, or a corporate practice, the feedback loop of the system's communications structure is remarkably similar. Diagrams 1 and 2 illustrate how either a private practice or a corporate organization or group practice can achieve the communications structure.

One of the principal benefits of a clinical services and records review system is that it provides a forum for establishing policies in an ongoing practice. An example of the system would be the establishment of a sample clinical records policy. The following mater. .l represents a policy statement that one could develop as a result of having such a system in place.

## SAMPLE CLINICAL RECORDS POLICY

A clinical record must be maintained for each person who has been seen as a client. The purposes of the clinical record are:

1. To provide a means of communication between the counselor and other professionals contributing to the client's care
2. To serve as a basis for planning individual client treatment
3. To furnish documentary evidence of the course of each client's illness and the treatment provided during each visit
4. To serve as a basis for analysis, study, and evaluation of the quality of care rendered to a client
5. To assist in protecting the legal interests of the client, the pastoral counselor, and the pastoral counseling organization
6. To provide clinical data for use in research and education

**DIAGRAM 1**
**Clinical Services Review Structure for Group Practice
or Corporate Organization**

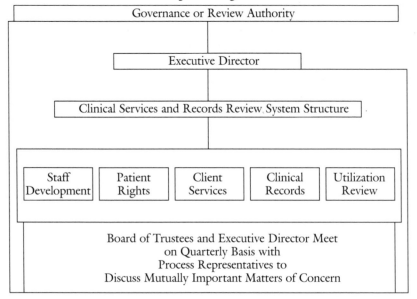

**DIAGRAM 2**
**Clinical Services Review Structure for Private Practice**

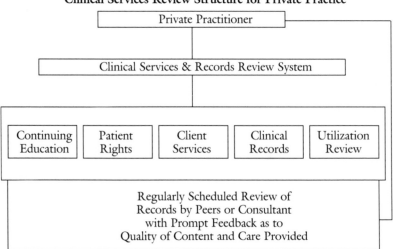

The clinical record is the who, what, why, where, when, and how of client care during a client visit. In order for the record to be complete, it must contain sufficient information to identify the client; to justify the pastoral care provided, including the diagnosis and treatment; and to record the results.

A family unit numbering system identifies each family involved in treatment. The family member numbering system identifies each client. All records are filed by terminal digit using a family number, then by numerical order using the member number. Appropriate nomenclature is then used to code all clinical procedures. As an example, the family unit number may be comprised of the first five letters of a family surname (for instance, LIBER—if less than five letters in surname, substitute with 0's); the family member number may be 1 for husband, 2 for wife, 3 for first sibling, 4 for second sibling, and so forth; and the terminal digit then includes the date first seen and the appointment number that day (for example, 12-1-92-04). Using the entire number would appear as follows: LIBER-2-12-1-92-04.

The clinical record is the property of the practitioner or clinic. The content of the record is the property of the client.

Hence no clinical information is released without the consent of the client, following the appropriate state law governing the release of such information. All clinical records are normally returned to their file at the end of each workday. Each record that leaves the clinic for any reason should be analyzed for accuracy before the record is refiled.

The attending provider must sign all correspondence before it is filed in the record. The person making the record entry must date and sign each one. All clinical encounters are reviewed against the clinical record for completeness and accuracy.

By using this policy statement, the individual counselor or organization assures that the information is both properly respected and reviewed for consistency and accuracy. In turn, this procedure provides a measure of protection if a claim is filed against a person providing pastoral care and treatment.

## EVERY ORGANIZATION NEEDS A FORUM

Both clinical organizations and individual practitioners can establish a committee process. Admittedly, the individual practitioner must be more creative to provide a forum to discuss the quality of a particular practice. But such a forum is an obligation as well as a necessity to assure that a practice is properly monitored and all results of practice are documented for review in case one needs to defend one's actions in a court of law.

# 4

# OVERSEEING ROLES
# AND RESPONSIBILITIES

In a pastoral counseling organization, the governing board, delegating the execution of its policies to the chief executive officer (CEO), accepts ultimate responsibility for standards of pastoral care provided, including both the quality assurance program and the clinical records system. In turn, the CEO should delegate the fulfillment of that responsibility to appropriate personnel as deemed necessary for the successful management of these processes. One should assign tasks to specific individuals and clearly delineate the roles of all persons involved. Open communication and cooperation between management and providers become essential components whenever a situation requires clarification. Those in private practice should also emphasize open and proper communication between the therapist and the individual responsible for carrying out the clinical records assignment.

One may use lay assessors for the abstraction (summarization) of charts and for other clerical tasks that may become necessary. Individuals in private practice may use peers or consultants who can provide the necessary follow-up information to assist in these clerical and administrative tasks.

One should have systems in place that permit one to study patterns of care in an efficient and effective manner. It is the responsibility of the CEO to assure that remedial actions are implemented and completed in a timely fashion.

Management can periodically conduct a quantitative analysis to assess client needs when clinical records are maintained using a code system. The quantification of such problems that counselors within a group practice address allows management to identify needs requiring particular counselor competency or the utilization of new techniques. The needs so identified are then assessed according to their relative importance and challenge or complexity to counselors. The highest priority needs become the subjects for which management can arrange continuing education for counselors, through the use of training sessions, seminars with specialists, films, or other resources.

The service delivery system within a PCO revolves around the interaction of an individual client with an individual counselor or groups of clients with teams of counselors. The counselor(s) is supported by a responsive team of ancillary personnel, who actually initiate care the moment the client enters the pastoral counseling center. Pastoral counselors treat all client communications confidentially; the client has a valid expectation of privacy. Whether the clergy-penitent privilege applies is a matter of state law and depends on a number of factors. Nonetheless, counselors must fulfill professional responsibilities during the course of therapy, and honoring these obligations need not compromise the confidential nature of the counselor-counselee relationship.

## RECEPTION COUNSELING

When the client first visits a PCO, a representative should interview the client or a responsible party and record pertinent information required to maintain a complete registration of that client within the computer or manual system of the practice. The interviewing counselor should be trained to assist in screening clients to identify emergent problems and to understand the requirements of third-party payments for which that client may qualify on either a full or partial basis. Clients with emergent medical or psychiatric problems should be registered only after a person medically trained to deal with such situations has treated them. If, in the view of the reception counselor, a medical triage of the client is necessary and is not available within the PCO, then that client should be referred outside the PCO to an organization with the ability to address that challenge.

### Utilizing Physician Services

Many pastoral counseling organizations utilize psychiatric physicians or family practitioners as consultants and ask the physician to be available to see a client requiring immediate care and treatment. Each physician should be consulted at any time the receiving counselor has doubts about the appropriateness of a treatment modality or perceives the need for immediate medical intervention.

### Handling Emergencies

In addition to a standard intake examination, any client entering pastoral care for a mental health need should show evidence of having had a complete medical examination within the past twelve months. If the client has not received a medical examination within that period, then as a matter of policy the client should be required to seek an independent medical evaluation by a licensed and board-certified physician sometime during the period of the first three visits.

### Referring for Specialty Care

All pastoral counseling organizations and private practitioners should retain a listing of medical and surgical specialists to whom they can refer for immediate care a client showing emergent symptoms. In all instances, any listing of physicians should include only certified specialists who have successfully completed the board examinations in their medical specialty.

### Following Up on Missed Appointments

Many providers feel that a client who does not meet an appointment bears the responsibility for that omission. In many instances, however, unless the provider has exerted and documented considerable effort to encourage the client to seek proper follow-up, the provider may be held responsible or negligent by a court for that client's failure to meet an appointment. Therefore the following procedure is recommended in order to ensure that the counselors protect themselves when a client does not meet a scheduled appointment.

1. Providers should document in the clinical record the type of follow-up they have recommended for each client.
2. At the end of each clinical day, someone from the PCO or practice should place no-show charts in an assigned box in the clinical record area. The boxes should be divided according to practitioner, and each practitioner should be responsible for assigning the appropriate notes indicating a failure to show for an appointment.
3. All no-show charts should be stamped with a "failure/cancellation" stamp, and broken appointments should be verified. If the client has cancelled or rescheduled, it should be indicated in the chart and no further action should be taken. In most instances, however, it is advisable for the provider or a designated representative to contact the client by phone or send a follow-up card by mail indicating the failure to show. This action should also be noted in the clinical record. The clinical record should then be returned to the system.

## RESPONSIBILITIES OF COUNSELORS

Each counselor has a responsibility to provide an entry in the clinical record on a timely basis, preferably immediately after providing a client with a service, and to sign or initial the record indicating that they have provided that service. Noting in the record such exceptions as a missed appointment is also the responsibility of the counselor. In addition, the counselor is responsible for communicating a client's emergent conditions to others within the system who can then address the immediate needs of that client. Assuring that information entered into the system is accurate represents an ongoing responsibility of each counselor. Finally, the counselor is responsible for reviewing the record and assuring that the progress notes are complete and accurate.

A designated person within the practice or PCO should be responsible for review of every clinical record that has been used on each day to assure that the appropriate entries are indicated and that the provider has signed or initialed the entry. If a record is incomplete, the designated person has the responsibility to seek out the counselor and ask that she or he update the record appropriately for closure and return it to the system.

# 5

## PROVIDING
## EMERGENCY COVERAGE

Every health care practice inevitably has clients with emotional and mental trauma that require emergency care and prompt follow-up in order to reduce the stress or anxiety associated with that occurrence. To address such problems, a PCO or individual pastoral counselor should have certain standards in place that facilitate a referral and maximize its chances of success.

In addition, counselors should have a means to refer clients promptly to an inpatient setting or an emergency room if the mental or emotional distress seems to reflect a physical problem or one that could involve hyperactivity or violence.

### STANDARD 15

PCOs or private practitioners who choose to provide some emergency services within their facilities should have a formally prepared and documented plan for the provision of such services.

*Methods of Compliance*
a. Assignment of staff responsibilities for key functions in an emergency
b. Written expectations of accountability for fulfillment of responsibilities in an emergency
c. Conduct mock drills with written evaluations of handling of emergency situations which are portrayed

To comply with this standard, the plan should include specific conditions that the client may face and the PCO's methods for addressing those conditions. The plan should also include referral arrangements through local acute psychiatric or general hospitals. In addition, the plan should describe transportation facilities for clients in an emergency condition, including the telephone numbers of the resources.

One should have provisions for physician consultation twenty-four hours per day, seven days per week; in addition, one should have provisions for a pastoral counselor to be available when a client requires immediate pastoral care or support therapy.

## STANDARD 16

Those who routinely provide emergency services should have a specific plan to provide referral and follow-up information to the client's primary counselor if other than the one the PCO employs or uses.

### Methods of Compliance

a. Chief executive officer responsibilities
b. Counselor responsibilities
c. Reception counseling responsibilities
d. Physician services responsibilities
e. Emergency services provider responsibilities
f. Responsibilities in effecting referrals for specialty care

To comply with this standard, the PCO should have available for review appropriate brochures or information that document the availability of services and verifies the capability of the PCO to provide that service.

## STANDARD 17

One should have a documented and written protocol for the authentication and filing of all reports and emergency mental health examinations performed on behalf of a client.

### Methods of Compliance

a. Document type of examination performed
b. Enter pertinent observations in client record
c. Document attempts to contact client's family or designated responsible person

A pastoral counselor or pastoral counseling organization should make this protocol available to any client who requests it. The action should be clearly documented in the clinical record.

This is particularly important in those instances in which the client's condition changes dramatically during the course of treatment. If a client is unable to recall such a request, a failure to properly document on the part of the practitioner may become a basis for litigation as well as a weakness in the defense of that claim.

## STANDARD 18

For clients with either mental or emotional trauma, one should have a procedure for documenting the trauma and for follow-up with an appropriate counselor who is able to sustain the treatment.

*Methods of Compliance*

a. Document specific occurrence of trauma and diagnosis
b. Document name and professional title of person designated to treat client
c. Document prognosis in wake of that episode

## STANDARD 19

Clearly define emergency services that will be provided within facilities.

*Methods of Compliance*

a. Preparation of a plan and notation of conditions under which the facility provides emergency services
b. Document procedures for providing specific emergency services in the facilities
c. Document names, addresses, and telephone numbers of outside referral resources
d. Document plan for transportation to outside referrals

## STANDARD 20

Provide a specific plan for filing all reports.

*Methods of Compliance*

a. Establish written expectations for documentation
b. Designate an office or person to receive reports
c. Stipulate time period for filing reports

## STANDARD 21

Establish a procedure for follow-up with counselor or with facility to which patient is referred.

*Methods of Compliance*

a. Establish tickler file for follow-up*
b. Designate office or person to handle follow-up
c. Document all attempts to follow-up and the results of those attempts

The importance of complying with the standards governing treatment or referral for mental and emotional trauma (Standards 18–21) should not be underestimated. First, and foremost, a practitioner or organization must recognize their limits of capacity to provide service in response to an emergent condition. Second, having in place a documented system of referral provides an immeasurable benefit to the patient as well as validating the good judgment of the provider. Finally, the ability to recognize need and complete the referral on a timely basis provides the most compelling evidence of responsible care when needed in a court of law.

Beyond its legal implications, meeting emergency needs represents a serious consideration of the PCO. It is essential that before advertising such services, the organization consider seriously its capability of fulfilling those services. If a client believes that the organization did not fulfill its promises and frustrated the client's expectations, it is not unusual for the client to seek legal redress. This situation then becomes another major challenge for the individual practitioner or organization in fulfilling the role and mission as a provider. Hence the watchword is caution as well as a realistic assessment of the capabilities of the organization and its permanent staff of counselors.

One gains nothing from overrepresenting availability of counseling services for which one has limited on-site capability. The risk of harm to others warrants a realistic approach, utilizing a referral mechanism to professionals who are more capable of providing the emergency services when necessary.

---

* Note: a tickler file customarily is organized chronologically by date and provides a reminder as to timing for follow-up action.

# 6

## KEEPING IN FORCE PROPER INSURANCE COVERAGE

The most important insurance coverage for a PCO or a private practice is professional liability insurance. But other insurance coverages form an integral part of the insurance management program of any PCO or individual practitioner, even though they do not provide the same level of protection.

### STANDARD 22

Each practitioner or PCO should have valid and collectible professional liability insurance in force.

*Methods of Compliance*
a. Maintain proper insurance in force
b. Carrier rated at least A*

### STANDARD 23

Each practitioner or PCO should have valid and collectible general liability insurance.

*Methods of Compliance*
a. Maintain proper insurance in force
b. Carrier rated at least A*

### STANDARD 24

Each PCO should have valid and collectible directors and officers liability insurance in force (incorporated counseling centers only).

---

* Note: Standards 22–27 reference among the methods of compliance the necessity of securing coverage from an insurance carrier rated A or better. This rating refers to the financial strength of the insurance carrier. The highest eligible rating for a carrier is A + +. The ratings are prepared annually by the A. M. Best Company of Oldwick, N. J.

*Methods of Compliance*
a. Maintain proper insurance in force
b. Carrier rated at least A*

## STANDARD 25

Each practitioner or PCO should have valid and collectible auto liability insurance in force.

*Methods of Compliance*
a. Maintain proper insurance in force
b. Carrier rated at least A*

## STANDARD 26

Each practitioner or PCO should have valid and collectible property insurance in force.

*Methods of Compliance*
a. Maintain proper insurance in force
b. Carrier rated at least A*

## STANDARD 27

Each practitioner or PCO should have valid and collectible workers' compensation insurance in force.

*Methods of Compliance*
a. Maintain proper insurance in force
b. Carrier rated at least A*

Organizations or individual practitioners can use several methods to manage the risks they face. It is first appropriate to define the meaning of the term *risk* as it pertains to the management of an insurance program. For our purposes, risk is "the possibility of financial loss due to contingency" (Vaughan 1986, 3). The situation and environmental conditions determine the description of risk management.

The element of risk originates from two sources as two distinct types—dynamic (speculative) and static (pure). Dynamic or speculative risk can create profits and losses and originates in business or investment activities. Static or pure risk can cause only losses and is a function of the insurance marketplace (Mehr and Hedges 1963, 89). In the context of this discussion, we need to consider only pure risk because it provides the most compelling rationale for proper risk and insurance management both for solo practitioners and PCOs.

Risk and insurance management programs have been in place for many years in the business and human services world. Industrywide use of the concept originated during the 1950s; it was called risk management during the early days (Dankmyer and Grow 1977, 51, 62–63).

The health field adopted individual portions of risk management as a concept until the late 1980s, and then only because managers found themselves in hopelessly complex dilemmas that they had never before experienced.

Today, the containment of insurance costs is vital to the fabric of an organization's ability to exist budgetarily—so much so that a broader approach to insurance and risk management has replaced the conventional wisdom of "cover it and forget it." This approach considers risk and insurance management as the reduction or elimination of an uncertainty of financial loss resulting from risks of a fortuitous nature (Wood 1975, 56).

Thus risk and insurance management is more than the management of malpractice or professional liability, because financial loss pertains not only to professional liability but also to workers' compensation, property preservation, and, in general, any and all potential losses of revenue. Although the primary area of risk and insurance management is professional liability, the pastoral counselor or PCO needs to consider other types of insurance coverages as well.

At the outset, each PCO that chooses to implement a program of risk and insurance management should employ the use of a risk management committee. Both the scope and function of the committee varies according to the size of the PCO. All staff groups should be represented on the committee. Even in small pastoral counseling organizations or solo practices, it is important to have a process, if not a committee, in place, to review the risks of liability periodically and regularly. In addition, it is most advantageous to have a designated legal counsel to consider pertinent issues of the practice that become a matter of concern.

Cost control is an important issue not only for large organizations but also for small organizations and individual practices. The review of liability exposures can assist both the private practitioner and the PCO in developing an overall cost-control program that minimizes expenses and maximizes the return to that organization or individual. According to Russell Gallegher (1956), a leading risk manager in the business world, cost control is the main function of risk management.

The management of risk seeks to control two kinds of costs associated with static or pure risks:

1. The costs of risks: The possibility that losses may occur is adequate to pro-

duce the costs of risks; one must acquire insurance whether or not the losses materialize.

2. The costs of losses: loss costs are evident when losses do materialize, and one must acquire insurance whether or not one accurately predicts the frequency and severity of losses. The fact that losses do materialize produces the costs (Mehr and Hedges 1963, 50).

After adopting a risk management process, one then implements a series of five procedures designed to assure that the organization or individual practitioner is doing everything possible in the area of risk control:

1. Identification of current and potential areas that can produce a loss. This is perhaps the most important and objective consideration in evaluating liability exposures. At the same time, it is probably the most difficult step in establishing a successful loss and cost-control program. The task is more complex for a corporate organization than for a solo practitioner because of the variety of persons working in the organization.

   This procedure indicates that loss control or risk management is not solely a reactive subject. It is a proactive process that provides an opportunity to eliminate the chances of loss before a loss occurs.

   Both solo practitioners and corporate organizations should use incident report forms. These forms provide an audit trail over an extended period of time that may yield cogent information in the event that one person or a series of particular events contributes to the incident reports. One may also use these forms to establish the defense of a person or organization if litigation ensues. In addition, such forms can assist in preventing many claims from even being filed, because they provide management with an opportunity to become aware of the situation, go back to the client, review possible corrective measures, and implement them to avoid a court appearance and the attendant costs.

2. Risk evaluation. Risk evaluation reviews and categorizes all the available incident reports for a period of at least six months. In addition, comparing data about accidents or incidents provides information about the severity and frequency of those incidents. One must evaluate each exposure to liability based on its full value, its maximum loss potential, or its impact on an organization. Then one must determine the replacement cost of that particular occurrence. For some items, such as buildings, this cost is a tangible measure that one can readily determine. For liability owing to an accident or professional incident, this evaluation provides more of a subjective measure of the potential costs to the provider.

3. Elimination of liability. After determining that a risk exists and evaluating it, one should view it as a persistent, serious threat. Most often, over a period of time the risk evaluation will reflect an aberration in a practitio-

ner's method of treating clients, and will provide an opportunity either to correct the problem or to remove the practitioner from those situations in which he or she has not demonstrated good judgment. For pastoral counseling organizations, this procedure is important because even if the efforts to eliminate a particular risk do not succeed, the fact that the organization has injected itself into the process and has attempted to ameliorate the problem provides substantial documentation that it has not been negligent in its management efforts. In court, then, this procedure can shift the burden of responsibility from the overall organization to the complainant.

4. Reduction of risk. Although many risks cannot be fully eliminated, the establishment of a risk management process provides an opportunity to reduce them to a level where they can be affordable and more predictable within the total scheme or realm of the organization's insurance program. In turn, this reduction minimizes both the probability or frequency of loss and the severity of such losses if they do occur. For example, one can probably not eliminate completely an exposure to loss from a fall on a stairway; but the addition of a handrail and nonskid tread strips may reduce significantly the probability and the seriousness of such a fall.

5. Transfer of risk. Risk transfer concerns basically those risks that one cannot effectively eliminate or reduce and cannot assume because of the magnitude of cost. Risk transference is generally accomplished through the purchase of coverage whereby commercial insurance assumes responsibility for particular insured incidents.

The remainder of this chapter addresses various mechanisms for transferring risk to fully insured programs in which the use of bona fide insurance carriers substantially minimizes the chance of financial ruin.

## CONSIDERING AN INSURANCE CARRIER

It is extremely important to consider the financial rating and stability of an insurance carrier. Indeed, the number of insurance companies that have gone out of business has provided substantial impetus for the careful consideration of factors that may affect the financial stability of an insurance company and the prudence of that carrier in handling the money that policyholders have entrusted to them.

Three primary sources or rating services evaluate insurance companies: A. M. Best Company, which for many years has served as the guidepost of the insurance industry; Standard and Poors, a noted rating service for businesses and commercial enterprises; and Moody's Investors Services, which also provides a rating service for businesses and other commercial enterprises. Through the use of these three rating services, individuals and organizations can gain a fair appraisal of the financial viability of the company with which they may choose to do business. Once one has decided that an insurance company or series of companies is acceptable, it then becomes the responsibility of the buyer of insurance to consider carefully the type of coverages to purchase.

## LIABILITY INSURANCE

Liability insurance comprises two primary areas of coverage: property damage and bodily injury.

Comprehensive general liability insurance (also known by the acronym CGL) protects one if a visitor slips or falls and incurs an injury. An incident resulting from a slip or fall may be defined as a sudden and unexpected occurrence that is definite in both time and location.

Professional liability insurance or malpractice coverage, which some call incorrectly an "errors and omission" policy, represents the professional interests of the pastoral counselor if charges of negligence or incompetence arise during the course of administering professional services.

The most important criterion for selecting professional liability insurance relates to the form of coverage under which the policy is written. These policies take two distinct forms. One is *claims made*, which provides coverage only for those claims filed while the policy is in force. If a claim is filed after the policy expires, the insurance company bears no responsibility for legal defense or for the payment of a judgment, unless the policyholder has purchased an extended reporting period endorsement, often known as tail coverage. The cost of tail coverage can be more than 200 percent of the premium during the final year of coverage.

Because claims made coverage provides insurance protection only for the incidents filed while the policy is in force, one can illustrate it as walking from one room to another in a large house and closing each door as one passes from room to room. Each room represents one year of coverage. As a policy matures and moves from room one to room two, all the exposures from room one accrue to room two along with any unrealized exposures. The net result is that one who is insured under a claims made form needs to be concerned about two elements of that coverage: first, to purchase tail coverage when the policy is either cancelled or expires and the insured person or organization moves to another company; second, to keep track of the aggregation of claims over an extended time. In general, if one has the same claims made policy for a period of four to five years, one should consider higher aggregate limits for that coverage than the original limits, because as the policy matures the aggregation of potential claim exposures can overwhelm the aggregate limits of coverage in a given policy year. Diagram 3 shows how claims may be apportioned in the event multiple claims are filed in one year under a claims made policy.

## DIAGRAM 3*
### Claims Made Form

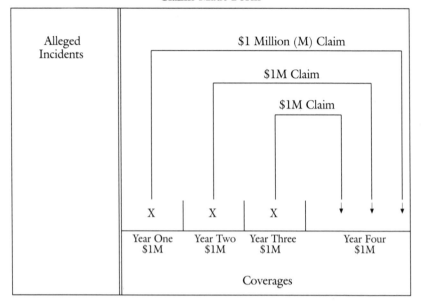

In diagram 3, three claims have been filed in year four for alleged incidents that took place in years one, two, and three.

Because this is a claims made form, all three claims and the resultant legal costs and awards are credited to the year four limits of liability. For example, because most insurance policies have a special sublimit, if the claims are for alleged acts of sexual impropriety, the insured could have as little as $25,000 per claim available for legal expenses and resulting judgments from each of the three claims.

One additional aspect of claims made coverage not reflected in diagram 3 is that a claims made policy normally has a five-to-eight-year period of maturation. During this period, the carrier adjusts the premium level to reflect the frequency and severity of claims and losses. If losses persist beyond the period, there is no guarantee that the premium will stabilize and level off. In other words, an insured sacrifices the period of time in which the carrier will accept responsibility for a loss and gains few material concessions in return. For individual private practice pastoral counselors, the effects could be significant and financially damaging, much more so than for a corporate organization or group practice.

Under an *occurrence form* of coverage, the person or organization is forever insured for the time period that a policy is or has been in force. Thus if a claim is filed several years after the policy has expired and the alleged incident oc-

---

* Note: Diagram presented to Aaron Liberman in personal communication from Edward T. Negley, M.D. (Cedar Grove, N.J., September, 1983).

curred during the time the policy was in force, the insurance company continues to bear a responsibility for legal defense or settlement of that claim. The occurrence form has two types of policy: the old occurrence form and the new occurrence form. Under the old occurrence form, the policy does not assign expenses such as legal defense costs as part of the policy limits. Under the new occurrence form, the insurance company amortizes the policy limits as a result of legal defense costs. This difference is an important consideration when purchasing an occurrence form of coverage because an expensive claim can deplete the policy limits before a judgment is even rendered. In addition, under the old or new occurrence forms of coverage, the aggregation of claims does not become an issue because even as the policy matures, the credit for claims filed is in the year that each incident is alleged to have occurred. Diagram 4 shows a significant point of contrast with the claims made policy.

**DIAGRAM 4\***
**Occurrence Form**

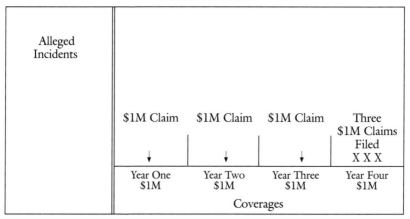

As in diagram 3, this policyholder has had three claims filed against him or her during year four. But because the policy has been written on an occurrence form, the claims and resulting judgments or legal expenses are credited against the respective years in which the incidents are alleged to have occurred. This comparison highlights a primary benefit of an occurrence form of coverage both while the policy is in force and beyond.

This comparison between occurrence form and claims made coverage is not intended to tout the former over the latter. In most instances the content

---

\* Note: Diagram presented to Aaron Liberman in personal communication from Edward T. Negley, M.D. (Cedar Grove, N.J., September, 1983).

of the two coverages differs little because most practitioners or organizations will probably never have to use the benefits of such coverage. In a society that emphasizes buyer beware (caveat emptor), however, it is important to note these differences in coverage; an informed consumer is less likely to be a surprised buyer at some future time. It is important to note also that the occurrence form of coverage may not be available under some circumstances, and purchasing a claims made policy with the knowledge of what to expect provides buyers with a better opportunity to select both the limits and the coverage that best suit their needs.

### Directors and Officers Liability

Directors and officers liability insurance (D&O coverage) provides protection for individual trustees in their capacity as policymakers on behalf of the organization named as the insured. D&O coverage under many home owner's policies is extended when an individual serves in a nonpaid capacity as a director or an officer of a nonprofit organization. Almost all D&O coverages are written on a claims made form, and some policies are written to protect the organization only from the exposures of individual directors. It is important for insureds to consider carefully the value of a policy that insures only the organization, because that coverage leaves the responsibility of individual protection to the individual director or officer. Coverage for both the individual directors and the corporate organization is generally called enhanced coverage, and it is somewhat more costly. It is essential that buyers be aware of the type of coverage they purchase.

The D&O contract generally has a retention factor. The retention factor is usually calculated per director and as an aggregate for the organization as a whole during the term of the contract. This means that within the term of the contract, the insurance company expects the organization to provide first dollar coverage up to the limits of the retention factor. The insurance company generally pays the expenses and then bills the insured for that portion considered to be the retention limits of the policy. For example, if a policy has a one million dollar limit per policy year, with a retention factor of $5,000 per director and $15,000 as an aggregate for all directors, the total out-of-pocket costs for a claim would not exceed $5,000, even if there are more than three members of the governing board.

### Umbrella Liability

Umbrella liability coverage is insurance over and above the basic limits of liability provided by the underlying liability policies (general liability, professional liability, and auto liability coverages). Some policies also extend coverage over the employer's liability section of a workers' compensation policy. If such a policy provides additional coverage over only one policy type (such as auto liability), it is commonly called excess coverage. Coordination of underlying and umbrella or excess coverages undoubtedly minimizes conflict in the event a claim is filed or a loss occurs.

## Automobile Liability

Auto liability and auto loss coverages are generally written together and constitute what is known as the standard auto policy. This policy provides basic protection from liability claims for bodily injury and property damage arising out of the ownership, operation, or use of an insured vehicle. In a corporate entity, the coverage extends to employees of that organization and any person operating the vehicle with permission from the named insured. It is essential to note that auto insurance covers the vehicle being operated. The driver receives protection as an extension of the fact that she or he is operating that vehicle. In short, auto insurance follows the car, not the driver.

Uninsured motorist coverage in effect makes the insurance carrier responsible up to the liability limits for any uninsured or hit-and-run motorist who strikes the operator or a passenger of an insured vehicle. In most jurisdictions today, underinsured motorist coverage is part of the uninsured motorist contract.

Medical payments coverage provides for the payment of reasonable medical expenses resulting from an accident involving an insured vehicle.

Collision coverage applies to direct accidental damage to the insured vehicle resulting from a collision. It is usually written with a deductible. It is advisable to reconsider the need for collision coverage after the vehicle is five years old because the blue book value of such a vehicle often does not warrant the continuation of collision coverage.

Comprehensive coverage addresses direct accidental loss or damage to the insured vehicle other than through a collision. Vandalism represents one of the losses under this coverage.

Towing and labor coverage pays for emergency repairs to or the towing of a stalled or damaged vehicle.

## PROPERTY INSURANCE

Property insurance is often purchased as part of a small business-office package that includes property coverage and general liability coverage for slips and falls. The property insurance policy contains fire and extended coverage and, in some instances, all risk protection on the building and its contents plus liability for slips and falls that occur on the premises. Many counselors believe they have purchased a property policy as part of their general liability coverage because most comprehensive general liability contracts have a property damage component. But this component refers only to property damage connected with a visitor's accident, not to damage as a result of fire or other natural occurrences.

For private practitioners or pastoral counseling organizations that have a substantial amount of equipment or furniture, or that own the facility in which they are located, the purchase of adequate property insurance is an important consideration to their ongoing financial stability.

## WORKERS' COMPENSATION INSURANCE

Workers' compensation insurance provides coverage for occupation-related injuries or diseases. The employer makes the payments in the form of premiums to the workers' compensation carrier. This represents Part A Coverage. Part B Coverage of workers' compensation insurance includes employer's liability insurance, from which an employee may recover damages caused by the employer's negligence in creating an unsafe workplace. As with other liability coverages, workers' compensation premiums have two major determinants: the frequency of claims and the severity of claims. These factors appear as an experience modification that adjusts the workers' compensation premium. An organization with positive claims experience customarily sees its premium reduced, while an organization with negative claims experience sees its premium increased. In some instances, because of lax safety procedures within an organization, the workers' compensation premium has caused organizations either to go out of business or to merge with other companies in order to modify their liability exposure.

## CRIME AND FIDELITY INSURANCE

Although not a common occurrence, some employees have stolen or diverted client revenues from their employer. The crime and fidelity coverage is designed to protect the employer from loss due to employee theft. To secure such coverage, and for the insurance to cover that exposure, the employer must commit to prosecute the perpetrator if an exposure occurs.

## SUMMARY

In general terms these coverages represent the options available to pastoral counseling centers and individual providers to protect them if a liability claim is filed against them or their organization. As previously noted, although the incidence of such claims is not significant it is sufficient to have warranted a multifold increase in the cost of coverage since the mid-1980s. Therefore each person in the practice of pastoral counseling, whether associated with a professional organization or an individual practice, should consider carefully both the probability of a loss occurring and the possibility of insuring against that loss through the purchase of liability insurance.

# 7

## ORGANIZING
## AN OFFICE AND
## PREPARING TO SUPERVISE

When a pastoral counselor decides to go into private practice, or a pastoral counseling organization is founded, one should make some basic provisions and commonly take a number of steps to assure that the practice starts out and proceeds on a proper footing. As a starting point, the PCO should have a short-range list of objectives, as well as a long-range plan. The short-range objectives should include projections of clinical hours, as well as a month-to-month cash flow budget for the practice. The long-range objectives should be complemented by a full operating budget, which is formulated on an accrual basis to account for peaks and valleys in developing its patient services, as well as a twelve-month cash budget that reflects the cash flow needs both during and beyond the developmental stages of the operation.

An integral part of staffing an office or an organization is an accurate prediction of staffing needs. On occasion, the dreams and hopes of the practitioner supersede good judgment. It is essential that one overcome such temptation; conservativism in the development of an operating budget and practice plan should be at the forefront of one's considerations. Recognizing that situations vary, one can alter the content and complexity of both the cash flow and accrual budget to meet the exigencies affecting each respective organization.

### FORMULATING A PRACTICE PLAN

As one develops a strategy for successfully implementing a pastoral counseling service, one should carefully consider some elements that go into the formulation of a practice plan.

#### Office Considerations

An office provides a means of articulating, at a subliminal level, the goal and direction of a pastoral counseling practice. Opulence and significant expense in decorating an office may fulfill an immediate need for self-recognition. In the long run, however, lavish expenditures can impede the success of a PCO.

Maintaining a tasteful, comfortable, yet subdued office environment seems preferable.

## Staffing Considerations

The receptionist/secretary is as important to a practice and its success as the practitioner. One should develop a profile of the type of person to fulfill that role, and if one is going to overspend by a significant amount in any category it should be in the wages of the receptionist/secretary. The person having the first point of contact with the patient, the family, and visitors to the office sets the tone as to how those persons view their experience when coming to that facility. Hence having a positive image at the front desk is crucial, and one should emphasize it in all budgeting and recruitment efforts.

## Clinical Staff

Hiring a clinical staff is much like entering marriage. If it works it can be fulfilling and beneficial to all parties concerned. If it does not work it can be a nightmare and representative of all problems that troubled relationships can engender. Thus one should select clinical staff persons with an eye toward conformance with the overall objectives of the PCO and a commitment on the part of those who join the organization or practice to fulfill all established requirements and standards of conduct. It is essential, therefore, that one thoroughly check the background of all prospective staff. If a prospective counselor does not have professional liability insurance in force and is not new to the pastoral counseling profession, one must raise serious questions as to why such coverage is not in force. Unsatisfactory or evasive answers to these questions should give one pause in hiring. Standard background checks with the prospective employee's professional association or society should include a review of any ethical breaches or investigations of practice violations. These checks are essential in establishing a relationship of trust among all practitioners.

## Contractual Agreement

In order to minimize misunderstandings from the outset of a relationship, it is advisable to enter into a service agreement or contractual relationship, which details the employer's expectations and answers the prospective employee's questions. To this end, it is most important that the contract provide measurable expectations, including the number of clinical service hours the provider makes available during the course of a workweek, and the requirements of the provider to maintain clinical records, to fulfill utilization review requirements, and to perform other administrative or clinical functions within the practice. If a prospective employee or contract staff member demurs at fulfilling the requirements and objectives articulated prior to commencing a work relationship, the prospective employer gains a better perspective of how the relationship may develop and even whether to enter that relationship. A written and signed agreement provides a more objective basis for establishing a working relationship, maintaining and rewarding the relationship, and, where necessary, ending such a relationship. It also affords a more focused basis for employment understandings.

## ESTABLISHING SUPERVISORY RELATIONSHIPS

In addition to the basic requirements of cooperation and working together in a supervisory relationship, it is quite important also to establish understandable yet firm direct clinical service production requirements for any person whom one supervises. At the outset, it is essential that both the supervisor and the person being supervised have professional liability insurance in force. Failure to require malpractice insurance can result in the supervisor being held financially accountable for the actions of the one being supervised.

Documenting each supervisory or training encounter is a significant requirement for a successful relationship. Indeed, it is one of the essential components of such a relationship, and one should neither overlook nor minimize its importance. One should at least discourage, if not preclude, isolated and unsupervised one-on-one counseling sessions between a person under supervision and a patient, until the person being supervised demonstrates the maturity, competence, and responsibility to handle such a situation. In terms of frequency, one should conduct the supervisory sessions at least weekly; from the outset, these sessions should include a basic understanding of what the supervisor will review and consider during their course.

*When a supervisory relationship exists, particularly if the supervisor is not directly involved in providing all relevant patient care, one should not permit billing of third-party payers. In a growing number of states there has been a prosecution of claims, as well as an initiation of criminal charges against persons providing supervision who then bill as though their office has provided the direct service. Although only isolated instances have occurred among those in the pastoral counseling professions, the results have been uniformly disastrous to the counselor's practice.*

Although the establishment of a pastoral counseling practice or a PCO can represent both a challenge and an opportunity for significant success, it also presents a potential mine field if the senior members of that practice do not have strict expectations and controls. Documentation may not be the most desirable of requirements, but it does indirectly contribute to bottom-line management (managing the profitability of an organization or private practice). It also provides a means of objectively establishing a clinical practice properly founded on the highest precepts of good business management and ethical requirements. The most important message of this chapter is that if one develops a measure of doubt in the course of negotiating a professional relationship, then one should carefully review and consider the advisability of consummating or continuing that relationship.

# 8

## REQUIRING
## WRITTEN CONSENT

One of the most important elements to assure adequate protection for a pastoral counselor against whom a claim is filed is the written consent form. Client consent in a human services setting is often thought to be superfluous because the client has usually requested pastoral care. Nevertheless, a client receiving services for which he or she has not given formal written consent may later file a liability claim against that organization. Therefore both individual practitioners and pastoral counseling organizations should use consent forms as a prerequisite to counseling services.

### TYPES OF CONSENT

Individual practitioners and PCOs should routinely use the following types of consent forms:

1. *Consent to counseling.* One should require each client to sign the consent to counseling form prior to receiving counseling services.
2. *Authorization for disclosure of information.* The client should sign this form and indicate to whom the counselor can provide information, specified by name of person or by title if it is an employee assistance program.
3. *Agreement to payment of fees for services rendered.* This form should specify precisely—to the penny—the cost of treatment and the terms for payment. Both the client and the counselor should follow to the letter the agreement to pay forms. As a counselor, one enters into a contract with the client to pay for services. If the client at some point declines to pay, or decides against paying for those services, then one should terminate counseling at that time, or discontinue it until management decides to continue services without charge (pro bono) or on a reduced fee basis. The agreement to pay form should clearly specify this condition.
   A client who simply no longer wishes to pay for treatment often files a claim against a counselor. It is also common for a client to demand restitution of funds paid for counseling and to file allegations that there was

no agreement before counseling began as to the charge for each office visit. By having an agreement to pay form completed, the counselor ensures that each client is aware of the cost of care. The counselor also thereby performs her or his duty to advise each client of the cost of counseling services.

Nonetheless, if a client wishes to discontinue counseling, expresses dissatisfaction with the service rendered, and demands a return of the funds paid, the counselor is often well advised to comply and simply terminate the service to that individual. In the long run, avoiding legal claims helps reduce the risk of future cancellation of one's professional liability coverage.

This book has provided a series of standards that individual pastoral counselors as well as those associated with PCO may follow to control effectively the incidence of liability and to assist in improving both clinical aspects and business practices associated with their program.

## SELF-ANALYSIS OF THE STANDARDS

As a reminder of these considerations, Appendix 1 summarizes the standards and the methods of compliance, and indicates the level of compliance or noncompliance with those standards. It should be emphasized that for the pastoral counselor or PCO to achieve an acceptable level of performance, the overall compliance average should be 90 percent; that is, one should affirmatively answer 90 percent of the standards and/or methods of compliance in order to reach an acceptable level of compliance with the standards as presented.

Although these standards are not perfect or infallible, pastoral counselors and PCO can achieve a credible level of accountability for their actions and a most acceptable rating index for the management of their practice if they adhere to and review these standards periodically.

In summation, we offer seven professional canons of pastoral counseling, which, if followed, reduce the vulnerability of a pastoral counselor to unwanted and unnecessary litigation.

1. Begin counseling with a realistic prognosis
2. Establish reasonable expectations
3. Allow and encourage discussion pertaining to the client's goals and expectations
4. Work toward an early resolution of the client's problems
5. Avoid personal entanglements
6. Require prompt compensation for services
7. Establish and maintain ground rules of therapy

# 9

---

# OBSERVING SEVEN
# PROFESSIONAL CANONS

The foreboding nature of the acronym based on the initial letter of each canon (BE AWARE) is meant to provide an opening admonition regarding both the responsibilities and the potential areas of liability exposure that can adversely affect pastoral counselors and PCOs. A person entering pastoral counseling as a profession may not even think about exposure to litigation. Nonetheless, the hazards of the profession have become all too apparent, and litigation has affected many unwary and unsuspecting counselors.

Responsible, cautious counselors can avoid litigation and even unnecessary exposure to its specter. To accomplish this objective and to provide the finest quality care within their capabilities, counselors must follow some basic tenets of practice.

## BEGIN COUNSELING WITH A
## REALISTIC PROGNOSIS

It is essential that the person beginning counseling receive the counselor's realistic assessment of the possibility for improvement in the condition from which the person suffers. Too many counselors today do not consider the implications and importance of handling that initial interview session in a professional manner. Pastoral counselors face the challenge of being providers of a service having implicit business standards while simultaneously gaining the client's personal trust. Trust depends on credibility; one earns credibility by honest and realistic assessments.

The period of counseling is not a time of unnecessary or inappropriate experimentation; it is a time to provide proper care that enhances the client's future welfare. Therefore a fair and honest prognosis provides the basis for both the expectation of improvement and the service or treatment provided during counseling. It is essential to discuss the treatment sequence with candor yet with a sensitivity to the client's ongoing needs. To do otherwise establishes a basis for misunderstandings that can grow to disagreement with the therapeutic approach in the future. A wrong start may even expose the counselor to an unwanted bout with attorneys and court appearances.

## ESTABLISH REASONABLE EXPECTATIONS

When a counselor provides a realistic prognosis, the client is in a position to establish reasonable expectations of her or his experience with that counselor. It is important that a pastoral counselor take special care to understand the client in order to determine proper and responsible care, develop a course of treatment, or initiate a counseling program. This care elicits appropriate expectations from the client.

One of the more important factors differentiating clinical pastoral counseling from other forms of ministerial assistance is payment: a pastoral counselor is paid to provide a mental health service to a client in a clinical and confidential relationship. Avoiding other kinds of relationships with a client keeps pastoral counseling as the exclusive basis for a pastoral relationship. It is therefore crucial that the pastoral counselor help the client develop attainable expectations.

To accomplish this goal requires patience and thoughtful understanding on the part of the counselor. In addition, the counselor must be sensitive to both the strengths and the limitations of the client. In so doing, the counselor provides a strong basis for the client to accept the treatment process and to develop mechanisms to overcome his or her problems.

## ALLOW DISCUSSION REGARDING EXPECTATIONS

How often have counselors thought that their knowledge and understanding of mental health care provided special insights into the needs and expectations of their clients, only to discover that their clients' thoughts revealed expectations significantly different from their own. It is essential—indeed, critical—to the successful completion of a therapeutic experience that the counselor permit and even encourage clients to express themselves meaningfully and to contribute to the establishment and achievement of their goals and expectations for the therapy process, with the counselor as the facilitator of that experience. Merely to engage in counseling as a process that the counselor intuitively believes to be proper, without discussing the intended direction of therapy with the client, can in many instances be the basis of the treatment's failure.

## WORK TOWARD EARLY RESOLUTION OF PROBLEMS

Cash flow and financial responsibility are part of the business operation of a clinical practice. A practice that one does not manage like a business in almost all instances is ultimately unsuccessful. But one should not prolong counseling unless it serves the clear clinical needs of the client. Limiting the number of office visits per month and instilling in the client a feeling of independence from the counselor are essential components in encouraging improved relationships within the client's family.

## AVOID PERSONAL ENTANGLEMENTS

Almost daily one hears of a human services professional taking advantage in some way of a client's trust. It is disturbing to note that persons in the pastoral professions are increasingly included in the litany of articles and accusations about the misbehavior of professionals charged with the care of others.

It is crucial that the counselor separate herself or himself from the personal problems of each client. If a counselor detects an attraction developing between himself or herself and a client, the counselor should immediately modify if not curtail the professional relationship. A counselor should not in any way fraternize with a client.

Pastoral counselors have argued with some emotion that they cannot simply turn off their personal relationships with clients. But no counselor should provide professional counseling services to a client and then expect to enjoy a nonprofessional, personal relationship with that client. Not only is an immediate referral indicated under such circumstances, but a professional review of one's malpractice exposure becomes essential. In the pastoral counseling profession, the nature of the relationship with the client differs significantly from that of a personal friendship. At the beginning of counseling pastoral counselors must establish and clearly articulate their behavior and demeanor so that clients know what to expect—achieving a level of trust is an exercise in holding and delegating power. Pastoral counselors enjoy a power imbalance tilted in their favor, and away from the clients. They must not abuse that power by developing code language, excessive loyalty mechanisms, or overly personal and inappropriate language or behavior.

Thus one should have no personal involvement beyond that which takes place within the counseling session as a professional relating to a client. A rule of behavior that every pastoral counselor should follow is no physical contact between the counselor and the client beyond a handshake. The counselor must not rationalize hugging, kissing, fondling, petting, or sexual intercourse as part of the therapeutic process. These actions simply are not part of counseling, pastoral care, or therapy and cannot be justified as such. Moreover, in these days and times of awareness, such behavior and actions can lead only to regret, intimidation, and ultimately legal action; and the counselor will undoubtedly be viewed as having unduly abused the power relationship that she or he has enjoyed with that client.

Thus far in the discussion sexual misconduct has connoted the ultimate result of an errant personal relationship between therapist and client. While such transgressions are most frequently portrayed by the news media, another serious but less publicized problem involves business and investment ventures which can evolve during the therapeutic relationship. A business deal that goes awry can precipitously define the failure of that professional relationship. Moreover, it almost surely will preempt any good that has resulted from the therapist's work.

Attempts by a practitioner to rationalize or explain such a contaminated relationship as 'wearing different hats' or not permitting personal and professional interests to interfere with one another represents naivete at best. Simply stated, it is not possible to maintain a professional relationship once personal considerations become the focus of that interaction. It does not work and cannot succeed, because the focus of concern will have shifted from treatment to economic survival.

## REQUIRE PROMPT COMPENSATION
## FOR SERVICES

Pastoral counselors provide needed and useful services to their clients. Thus the client must understand and respect the business nature of the relationship. In order to achieve that goal it is essential that the pastoral counselor require prompt compensation for services rendered; clients should make all payments for services either immediately before or after a therapeutic session. There should be no grace period, because the importance of paying for that professional care and treatment diminishes considerably with the passage of even short periods of time. If payment is not received immediately before or after the next session, treatment should be curtailed until such time as payment is made.

## ESTABLISH AND MAINTAIN GROUND RULES

Every client should understand at the outset the counselor's expectations of the client's demeanor and behavior during therapy sessions. If some types of behavior particularly alienate a counselor, the counselor should inform the client at the outset, because this information provides the client with a basis of understanding the behavioral limits. If the client then does not feel that working with a particular counselor would be either satisfying or successful, it is best that the client seek the services of another professional whom the client perceives as more attuned and responsive to her or his particular needs.

As with professionals in any business, it is necessary that counselors reduce to writing some aspects of the professional business relationship in order to properly apprise recipients of the counselors' expectations and also to assure a clear understanding as to what will take place during the course of treatment. Therefore we strongly recommend that counselors prepare a memorandum of understanding for each client that clearly delineates the expectations of the counselor, with space provided for clients to insert their comments about how they wish to be treated.

In essence, we recommend the establishment of professional relationships based upon openness, candor, and honesty between the counselor and the client. Not establishing a forthright relationship at the outset affords too many opportunities for failure during the period of counseling, and these can only serve to diminish the value of treatment and the opportunity for successfully intervening in the problems that initially brought the client to the counselor.

It is essential that the counselor maintain honesty and integrity as the ultimate standard to which both their professional ideals and their counseling service aspire.

# APPENDIX 1

## SUMMARY OF STANDARDS AND METHODS OF COMPLIANCE

| Standard | Methods of Compliance | Status of Compliance |
|---|---|---|
| | | C-Compliant |
| | | NC-Noncompliant |

### PART A: QUALITY ASSURANCE PROGRAM

**Standard 1**

Ongoing Quality
Assurance Program

a. Review annually and monitor clinical practices
b. Review annually and evaluate clinical service policies
c. Modify clinical service policies as needed

**Standard 2**

Method for Information
Collection & Review

a. Clear statement of the purpose of care for each client
b. Profile of significant characteristics requiring modification for each client
c. Maintainance of standard information checklist for all clients seen in therapy
d. Name of referral source used when deemed appropriate

**Standard 3**

Written Protocol for
Improvement of Client
Care Quality

a. Involvement of colleagues
b. Presentation of clearly defined objectives

**Standard 4**

Documented Clinical
Oversight

a. Patient care committee or peer review
b. Status of problems identified and followed
c. Communication between reviewer and counselor
d. Scope and effectiveness of QA assessed annually
e. Inadequacies corrected

| *Standard* | *Methods of Compliance* | *Status of Compliance* |
| --- | --- | --- |

**Standard 5**

Demonstration of High-Quality Care

a. Consistent with principles of professional practice
b. Reflect concern for acceptability, accessibility, and availability of services
c. Description of system for providing services
d. SOP available for referral in an emergency
e. SOP for informing counselee of persons providing care
f. Demonstration of use of all diagnostic procedures
g. Documentation of availability of consultation
h. All information part of permanent clinical record

**Standard 6**

Documentation of Continuity of Care

a. Evidence of timely follow-up
b. Consistent use of treatment plan
c. Consistent use of patient consent form
d. Consistent use of problem list

**Standard 7**

Concern for Minimizing Cost of Care

a. Studies of treatment relevance
b. Studies of treatment timeliness
c. Studies of treatment effectiveness
d. Studies of duplication of services provided
e. Studies of cost effectiveness

**Standard 8**

Quarterly Quality Assurance Meetings

a. Sharing of views
b. Minutes documenting each meeting
c. Correction of improper treatment techniques
d. Persistent efforts to improve quality of care

| *Standard* | *Methods of Compliance* | *Status of Compliance* |
| --- | --- | --- |

## PART B: CLINICAL RECORDS

**Standard 9**

Maintain Accurately
Documented Clinical
Records Systems

a. Standardized records format
   for all counselees
b. Parameters set for collection
   and retention of information
c. Standardized procedures for
   retrieval of information
d. System to protect clinical
   records from loss, alteration,
   destruction
e. Designation of staff member
   to maintain and secure records
f. Standard data collection and
   retention policy

**Standard 10**

Provision for
Accurate
Documentation of
Record Content

a. Treatment progress duly
   noted
b. Timely updating of records
c. Attending clinician signs and
   dates entry
d. Note entry on problem list
   when appropriate

**Standard 11**

Clinical Records
System
Standardized

a. Client biographical
   information
b. Registration form
c. Consent form
d. Release of information form
e. Diagnosis
f. Ongoing problem list
g. Progress notes
h. Consultant reports
i. Medical examination report

**Standard 12**

Written Policy
Statement Requiring
Standard Clinical
Record Format

a. Clearly stated and unequivocal
b. Requirement of consistent
   format
c. Implications of not following
   policy requirements

| Standard | Methods of Compliance | Status of Compliance |
| --- | --- | --- |

**Standard 13**

Clinical Reports a
Permanent Part of
Clinical Record

a. Retain at least 7 years
b. Information treated as confidential
c. Consistent filing system for active and inactive clients

**Standard 14**

Clinical Records
Review Process

a. Utilization review process
b. Client services review process
c. Clinical records review process
d. Staff development/continuing education
e. Patient rights program

**Standard 15**

Emergency Services
within Facilities

a. Assignment of staff responsibilities in an emergency
b. Written expectations of accountability
c. Conducting mock drills

**Standard 16**

Referral & Follow-up
Information to
Primary Counselor

a. CEO responsibilities
b. Counselor responsibilities
c. Receptionist responsibilities
d. Physician responsibilities
e. Emergency services provider responsibilities
f. Referrals for specialty care

**Standard 17**

Protocol for
Authentication of
All Reports and
Examinations

a. Document type of examination
b. Enter pertinent observations
c. Document attempts to contact client family or responsible person

**Standard 18**

Procedure for
Documenting
Trauma and
Follow-up

a. Document occurrence of trauma and diagnosis
b. Document name and professional title of clinician providing treatment
c. Document prognosis

| *Standard* | *Methods of Compliance* | *Status of Compliance* |
| --- | --- | --- |

**Standard 19**

Define Services to
be Provided

a. Plan and conditions under which emergency services are provided
b. Document procedures for providing emergency services
c. Document outside referral resources
d. Document transportation plan

**Standard 20**

Specific Plan for
Filing All Reports

a. Written expectations for documentation
b. Designated office or person to receive reports
c. Stipulate time period for filing reports

**Standard 21**

Procedure for
Follow-up with
Counselor or Facility
Receiving a Referral

a. Tickler file for followup
b. Designate person or office to handle followup
c. Document all attempts to followup and results of those attempts

## PART E: PROPER INSURANCE COVERAGE

**Standard 22**

Professional Liability
Insurance

a. Maintain proper insurance in force
b. At least an A rated carrier

**Standard 23**

General Liability
Insurance

a. Maintain proper insurance in force
b. At least an A rated carrier

**Standard 24**

Directors and
Officers Liability
Insurance (Incorporated
Counseling Centers
Only)

a. Maintain proper insurance in force
b. At least an A rated carrier

| *Standard* | *Methods of Compliance* | *Status of Compliance* |
| --- | --- | --- |

**Standard 25**

Auto Liability
Insurance

a. Maintain proper insurance in force
b. At least an A rated carrier

**Standard 26**

Property Insurance

a. Maintain proper insurance in force
b. At least an A rated carrier

**Standard 27**

Workers'
Compensation
Insurance

a. Maintain proper insurance in force
b. At least an A rated carrier

# APPENDIX 2

## SAMPLE OF COMPLETED STANDARDS CHECKLIST

Organization or
Practitioner (if solo practitioner) __XYZ Pastoral Counseling Ctr.__
Name of Person Completing Checklist __Jane Doe__
Note: Insert number of methods compliant or noncompliant.     Date __8/25/92__
If standard is not applicable, please insert check mark in "NA" box.

| Standard 1 Ongoing Quality Assurance Program | Compliant 2 | No. of Methods 3 | Plan or Action |
| | Noncompliant 1 | NA ☐ | (a) Modified service policies scheduled for each 6-mo. period. (b) Process to commence Sept. 1, 1993. |

| Standard 2 Method for Information Collection & Review | Compliant 4 | No. of Methods 4 | Plan or Action |
| | Noncompliant 0 | NA ☐ | Fully compliant. |

| Standard 3 Written Protocol for Improvement of Client Care Quality | Compliant 3 | No. of Methods 4 | Plan or Action |
| | Noncompliant 1 | NA ☐ | (a) Statement of purpose being rewritten. (b) Will be completed Oct. 1, 1993. |

| Standard 4 Documented Clinical Oversight | Compliant 1 | No. of Methods 2 | Plan or Action |
| | Noncompliant 1 | NA ☐ | (a) Annual review of QA program effectiveness to be undertaken. (b) Reviewed in February each year. |

| Standard 5 Demonstration of High-Quality Care | Compliant 6 | No. of Methods 8 | Plan or Action |
| | Noncompliant 2 | NA ☐ | (a) SOP established to facilitate referrals in emergencies by Oct. 1. (b) Missing record info in place by Sept. 1, 1993. |

| Standard 6 Documentation of Continuity of Care | Compliant 3 | No. of Methods 4 | Plan or Action |
| | Noncompliant 1 | NA ☐ | (a) Treatment plans absent from 8 of 50 records reviewed. (b) Noted in records and clinics advised treatment plans due by Sept. 1, 1993. |

| Standard 7 Concern for Minimizing Cost of Care | Compliant 4 | No. of Methods 5 | Plan or Action (a) Studies of cost-effectiveness are being completed. |
| | Noncompliant 1 | NA | (b) Will be available for review Oct. 1, 1993. |

| Standard 8 Quarterly Quality Assurance Meetings | Compliant 4 | No. of Methods 4 | Plan or Action Fully compliant. |
| | Noncompliant 0 | NA | |

| Standard 9 Accurately Documented Clinical Records System | Compliant 5 | No. of Methods 6 | Plan or Action (a) Establishing standardized records format for all clients. |
| | Noncompliant 1 | NA | (b) Final format to be submitted for full staff review Oct. 1, 1993. (c) Implemented Nov. 1, 1993. |

| Standard 10 Provision for Accurate Documentation of Record Content | Compliant 3 | No. of Methods 4 | Plan or Action (a) Progress notes on each client visit to be required at all clinics. Written policy drafted by Sept. 1, 1993. |
| | Noncompliant 1 | NA | |

| Standard 11 Clinical Records System Standardized | Compliant 9 | No. of Methods 9 | Plan or Action Fully compliant. |
| | Noncompliant 0 | NA | |

| Standard 12 Standard Clinical Record Format | Compliant 2 | No. of Methods 3 | Plan or Action (a) Prepare clearly stated policy. (b) Policy completed by Sept. 1, 1993. |
| | Noncompliant 1 | NA | (c) After review by clinical staff, final policy implemented Oct. 1, 1993. |

| Standard 13 Clinical Reports a Permanent Part of Clinical Record | Compliant 2 | No. of Methods 3 | Plan or Action (a) Prepare policy statement requiring record retention for 7 yrs. |
| | Noncompliant 1 | NA | (b) Policy completed by Sept. 30, 1993. (c) Implemented by Dec. 1, 1993. |

| Standard 14 Clinical Records Review Process | Compliant 5 | No. of Methods 5 | Plan or Action Fully compliant. |
| | Noncompliant 0 | NA | |
| **Standard 15** Emergency Services within Facilities | Compliant 3 | No. of Methods 3 | Plan or Action Fully compliant. |
| | Noncompliant 0 | NA | |
| **Standard 16** Referral & Follow-up Information to Primary Counselor | Compliant 6 | No. of Methods 6 | Plan or Action Fully compliant. |
| | Noncompliant 0 | NA | |
| **Standard 17** Protocol for Authentication of Reports & Examinations | Compliant 3 | No. of Methods 3 | Plan or Action Fully compliant. |
| | Noncompliant 0 | NA | |
| **Standard 18** Procedure for Documenting Trauma & Follow-up | Compliant 2 | No. of Methods 3 | Plan or Action (a) Designation of person to be made by Sept. 1, 1993. (b) Written and measurable expectations of designee in place Oct. 1, 1993. |
| | Noncompliant 1 | NA | |
| **Standard 19** Define Services to be Provided | Compliant 3 | No. of Methods 4 | Plan or Action (a) Formal referral agreements will be executed by Oct. 1, 1993. |
| | Noncompliant 1 | NA | |
| **Standard 20** Specific Plan for Filing All Reports | Compliant 3 | No. of Methods 3 | Plan or Action Fully compliant. |
| | Noncompliant 0 | NA | |

| Standard 21<br>Procedure for<br>Follow-up with<br>Clinician/Facility<br>to Which Patient<br>Referred | Compliant<br><br>2<br><br>Noncompliant<br><br>1 | No. of<br>Methods<br>3<br><br>NA | Plan or Action<br><br>(a) Follow-up policy for all<br>referrals will be in place by<br>Oct. 1, 1993. |
| --- | --- | --- | --- |
| Standard 22<br>Professional<br>Liability<br>Insurance | Compliant<br><br>2<br><br>Noncompliant<br><br>0 | No. of<br>Methods<br>2<br><br>NA | Plan or Action<br><br>Fully compliant. |
| Standard 23<br>General Liability<br>Insurance | Compliant<br><br>2<br><br>Noncompliant<br><br>0 | No. of<br>Methods<br>2<br><br>NA | Plan or Action<br><br>Fully compliant. |
| Standard 24<br>Directors/Officers<br>Liability<br>Insurance<br>(Pastoral Counseling<br>Centers Only) | Compliant<br><br>2<br><br>Noncompliant<br><br>0 | No. of<br>Methods<br>2<br><br>NA | Plan or Action<br><br>Fully compliant. |
| Standard 25<br>Automobile<br>Liability<br>Insurance | Compliant<br><br>2<br><br>Noncompliant<br><br>0 | No. of<br>Methods<br>2<br><br>NA | Plan or Action<br><br>Fully compliant. |
| Standard 26<br>Property<br>Insurance | Compliant<br><br>2<br><br>Noncompliant<br><br>0 | No. of<br>Methods<br>2<br><br>NA | Plan or Action<br><br>Fully compliant. |
| Standard 27<br>Workers'<br>Compensation<br>Insurance | Compliant<br><br>2<br><br>Noncompliant<br><br>0 | No. of<br>Methods<br>2<br><br>NA | Plan or Action<br><br>Fully compliant. |

## COMPLIANCE SCORES FOR
## SAMPLE CHECKLIST

*Percentage of Compliance with standards:*

Fully Compliant with 14 Standards (52%)
Partially Compliant with 13 Standards (48%)
Completely Noncompliant with 0 Standards (0%)

Acceptable score is a minimum of 24 of 27 standards fully compliant (89%)

*Percentage of Compliance with methods of compliance:*

Fully Compliant with 87 methods (86%)
Noncompliant with 14 methods (14%)

Acceptable score is a minimum of 91 of 101 methods fully compliant (90%)

Note: To correct for margin of error created by having all standards of equal value, person or organization completing standards checklist will be deemed to have attained an acceptable score if 89% or better is achieved on standards compliance or 90% is achieved on methods of compliance.

# APPENDIX 3

# PROCESS FOR
# IMPLEMENTING STANDARDS

### STAGE ONE

1. Development of standard forms to be used by clinicians providing direct patient services.
2. These forms should include the following:
   a. Clinical record format
   b. Utilization review form
   c. Quality assurance audit checklist

### STAGE TWO

1. Meetings between management and staff to establish clinical practice ground rules for the use of the forms and the implementation of the process.
2. Input of clinical staff in these meetings is essential to reduce resistance to positive change.

### STAGE THREE

1. Follow-up training sessions for the purpose of assuring that all clinical persons understand and are able to use the standard forms.
2. Once again, staff input should be actively solicited.

### STAGE FOUR

1. At least quarterly quality assurance or utilization review meetings to assure staff compliance with required standards of clinical practice.
2. Outside speakers with expertise in this process can provide motivation and impetus for change.

### STAGE FIVE

1. Focused meetings with clinicians to correct technical problems that may be impeding compliance with standards of practice.
2. Resistance to change almost always includes fear as a factor. It therefore becomes important that one encourage staff members to confront their inability or unwillingness to change.

### STAGE SIX

1. Establishment of continuing education program to concentrate on particular areas of concern. The following are some topical areas that may merit consideration and attention:
   a. Importance of signed forms acknowledging consent to treatment
   b. Importance of maintaining timely client progress notes
   c. Importance of protecting confidentiality of client information
   d. Importance of knowing when to refer clients to an outside resource for acute or emergency follow-up
   e. Importance of documenting no-shows
   f. Importance of ongoing follow-up with active clients

2. Each continuing education module should be designed to enhance the knowledge of practicing clinicians. It also should provide a feedback loop to afford the recipient an opportunity to respond constructively to the continuing education experience.

## STAGE SEVEN

1. Regularly scheduled opportunities for staff members to offer constructive input to improve the program, particularly its specific elements.
2. Because pastoral counseling is a dynamic and constantly evolving discipline, it is essential that one have timely opportunities to effect needed changes in the programs. One should define a process that at least annually allows for suggestions to modify the methods of managing the administrative and quality assurance components of clinical practice.

# APPENDIX 4
# SAMPLE POLICIES AND PROCEDURES

## FILING AN INCIDENT REPORT

### Recommended Definition of an Incident

An incident is an unusual event involving a client or visitor that transpires in, on, or about the premises of the facility, or an unusual event occurring away from the premises but that is the result of an occurrence on the premises. The event is considered unusual if the result was unexpected, unintended, or undesirable.

### When to Complete an Incident Report

The responsibility for completing an incident report rests with any staff member who witnesses, discovers, or has direct knowledge of an incident.

In general, one must file an incident report for any of the following circumstances:

1. A disturbance that may interfere with normal day-to-day functions or that may affect the community standing of the practice
2. A significant abridgment of established policy or procedure
3. An event that is not a natural consequence of treatment or a patient procedure
4. An unusual event that may result in personal or bodily injury
5. Threat or announcement of intent to file an action or actual commencement of legal action relating to treatment provided
6. Any threat of personal harm or injury voiced by a client, visitor, or family member that requires precautionary measures
7. Failure to obtain proper consent for treatment or release of confidential information
8. Failure to release from treatment a client who has requested said release
9. Utilization of unauthorized restraint or seclusion in violation of established legal code
10. Any staff member's observed or alleged physical abuse of a client
11. Any alleged sexual, personal, or financial relationship between a staff member and a client currently being treated or within two years of discharge from treatment
12. The following client behaviors: self-inflicted injury, attempted suicide, injury of an employee, or injury to another client

### Timeliness of Report Completion

1. Responsibility for completing an incident report rests with any staff member who observes, discovers, or has direct knowledge of an incident.
2. The staff member should complete the incident report immediately, or at least before leaving the premises that day.
3. Any incident involving voiced hostility by a client, visitor, or family member requires immediate verbal communication to the director or senior person on duty, in addition to completion of an incident report.
4. Any additional staff member witnessing an incident is required to submit a supplemental incident report or a narrative statement of facts before leaving the premises that day.

CONFIDENTIAL REPORT of INCIDENT (not part of clinical record)

Name of Organization
or Practice: _____

Address: _____

Name of Person
Completing Report: _____ Telephone: _____

| Incident Date | Identification | Sex | Age | Type of Event | Time of Incident |
|---|---|---|---|---|---|
| | ☐ Client<br>☐ Employee<br>☐ Visitor | ☐ Female<br>☐ Male | | ☐ Slip/Fall<br>☐ Altercation<br>☐ Treatment/Testing | |

| Location of Incident | Nature of Injury |
|---|---|
| Was furniture or equipment involved?<br>☐ Yes ☐ No<br>☐ Admin. Offices ☐ Parking Lot/<br>☐ Reception     Sidewalk<br>☐ Corridor/ ☐ Treatment Office<br>   Stairway ☐ Other<br>☐ Elevator     (describe)<br>☐ Interior Premises _____<br>_____ | (Injury sustained as a result of incident)<br>(Check as many as apply)<br>☐ Contusion, ☐ Fatality<br>   Laceration, Abrasion ☐ Fracture/<br>☐ Concussion     Dislocation<br>☐ Corneal Abrasion ☐ Self-Inflicted Injury<br>☐ Puncture Wound ☐ No Apparent Injury<br>☐ Sprain/Strain ☐ Tooth Broken/<br>☐ Other (describe)    Chipped |

Explanation of Occurrence

Name of Client: _____

Principal Diagnosis: _____

Insurance
     ☐ Medicaid
     ☐ Medicare
     ☐ Private
     ☐ Other
     ☐ None

Occurrence (describe briefly): _____
_____
_____
_____
Counselor: _____
Involved Personnel: _____

Other Resulting Occurrences

☐ Against Clinical Advice      ☐ Expressed Dissatisfaction
☐ Client Property Missing/Damaged      ☐ Violated Rules

Did Client/Family Express Dissatisfaction?    ☐ No   ☐ Yes (describe complaint)
_____
_____

Names of Witnesses (include other patients or visitors): _____
_____
_____

Person(s) Accompanying Client: _____

Signature of Person
   Preparing the Report: _____

                     Date/Time: _____

## Procedure for Completing Incident Reports

1. The incident report should be completed as thoroughly as possible.
2. The report should be legibly written and signed by the person completing the report.
3. More than one block is often applicable in a given section. Each section should be read completely and all applicable boxes checked.
4. The report should be objective and factual. One should not record impressions or judgments. One must identify all persons by name or title.
5. Additional sheets may be attached for narratives or information provided by other witnesses if needed. Information contained in an addendum should be factual.
6. The name and complete address of all witnesses should be recorded.
7. Signatures must be legible and all reports dated correctly.
8. Completed incident reports and attachments should be retained in a secure place. Unless the report deals specifically with a care/cure issue, it should be maintained separate from the clinical record.

The following provides a section-by-section description of how one should complete the incident report.

*Clinic Information.* One should give the complete name of the organization or practice, mailing address, and contact person. Unless otherwise indicated, one should assume that the director is the contact person.

*Occurrence Information.* One should enter the date the incident occurred; and identify the complainant as a client, employee, or visitor; and list the complainant's gender and age. One should also indicate the type of incident and the time at which the incident occurred.

*Location of Incident and Nature of Injury.* These two categories more closely identify the event and the results. One should check as many boxes in each category as apply.

*Explanation of Occurrence.* One should record the client's full name and the reason why he or she is being seen as a client. One should check the appropriate box to indicate whether the client is covered under an insurance policy or is being seen on a private pay basis.

One should briefly describe the occurrence. If more space is needed, one can write on a separate sheet and attach it to the incident report form. One must provide factual information and be nonjudgmental in choice of words.

One should indicate the name of the attending counselor at the time of the occurrence, and write down the names of any personnel who were present at the time.

*Other Resulting Occurrences.* By checking one or more boxes, one should indicate if the client discontinued treatment against clinical advice, expressed dissatisfaction, lost or sustained damage to personal property, or violated center/practice rules.

If the client or family has verbally expressed dissatisfaction, one should give the name(s) and the nature of the complaint, stating factually what was said, in nonjudgmental language. One should clearly indicate quotations by the use of quotation marks.

Names of witnesses would include any other patients or visitors who witnessed the incident. The names of the clinic personnel who witnessed the incident should have been listed under "Involved Personnel" in the section on Explanation of Occurrence. One should also indicate the name(s) of anyone who accompanied the client and her or his relationship to the client.

Signatures, if not legible, should be accompanied by printed names. The incident report should be completed during the calendar day of the occurrence, if possible; if that is not possible due to the unavailability of witnesses, the report should be completed as early as it becomes practicable. In no event should completion of the incident report be delayed more than 72 hours from the time of occurrence.

## QUALITY ASSURANCE AUDIT

**A. Selecting Samples** (Samples refers to clinical records selected for audit purposes.)
1. Any time or demographic constraints should be outlined for each sample before record selection.
2. Each sample size should be approximately 50 records (no less than 25 records) for each audit topic.
3. Each sample should be either randomly or systematically selected.
4. Each sample should include all providers currently practicing at the center.
5. Charts used in the sample should include clients currently being seen by the respective providers.
6. The sample may be retrospective, concurrent, or prospective.
7. The sample selection process should consume as little time as possible.
8. Potential sources for selection of samples are:

   a. Computer printouts
   b. Encounter forms
   c. Claims or billing forms
   d. Card files
   e. Appointment lists
   f. Provider-generated lists

**B. Developing Criteria**
1. Criteria are measures by which one may evaluate care.
2. The establishment of compliance levels turns the criteria into standards or expected performance levels.
3. Explicit, generally applicable criteria lists that have critical elements of care for a particular audit topic.
4. Conditional or sequential criteria are developed to take into account variability or alternate paths for particular subgroups or individuals.
5. Criteria should be:

   a. *Objective:* sufficient precision and detail to make them relatively immune to varying interpretation by different individuals
   b. *Verifiable:* points on which they rest can be verified by consultation or documentation
   c. *Uniform:* independent of factors like size or location of center, qualification of

provider, or social and economic status of patient
d. *Specific:* specific for each type of condition evaluated.
e. *Pertinent:* should be relevant to the ultimate aim of the treatment being evaluated
f. *Acceptable:* should conform with generally accepted standards of good quality and be agreed upon by staff
g. *Explicit:* definite and clearly stated (as opposed to something implicit or assumed)
h. *Feasible:* capable of being applied in an efficient and effective manner
i. *Comprehensive:* looks at the total care given to the patient and takes into consideration the role of ancillary services

C. **Abstracting**
1. One should interpret whether charts meet respective criteria when it is not immediately evident that they do. This person may vary from audit to audit but should be present and available during the course of conducting and reviewing the audit for which they are responsible.
2. If criteria are unclear when abstraction begins, one should seek clarification before proceeding with the entire sample.
3. If more than one person is abstracting records, one must make sure that all abstractors interpret criteria consistently.
4. The abstract sheet should mimic criteria statements and be designed in an easily utilized check-off format.
5. The abstract sheet should include spaces for the client chart number, provider name, and age and gender of the client.
6. One should note on the abstract sheet when criteria are not applicable, or it is unclear whether criteria are met, so that the chart does not need to be pulled again for review.

D. **Compiling Results and Analyzing Problems**
1. One should tally and present results in a format that one can readily understand.
2. One should compare results for each criterion with expected performance or desired compliance levels.
3. One should pursue problem analysis for criteria that show a substantial difference between actual results and expected performance levels.
4. The audit committee should identify and agree on probable causes of problems.
5. Some performance deficiencies may be attributable to:
   a. Gaps in provider skills or knowledge
   b. Obstacles in the environment (e.g., inadequacies in various operational systems)
6. The committee should generate proposed solutions to problems, and then select solutions with the highest probability of success.

E. **Remedial Action**
1. Remedial actions should be specific, assign responsibility for each specified action, and establish a target date for completion. For example:

| *Deficiency* | *Specific Action* | *Target Date* | *Person Responsible* |
|---|---|---|---|
| Providers do not request return of clients for follow-up | Instruct providers to request follow-up and note in chart | 10/1/93 | Director |

| Clients do not return for appointments even when requested to do so | Design postcard reminder system | 9/1/93 | Administrative Assistant |

2. One should define the most feasible type of action. Specifically, one should choose a strategy that is:
   a. simplest to implement
   b. inexpensive to mount
   c. expedient
   d. most effective for achieving long-term results
3. Providers should rectify individual clinical record deficiencies when possible.
4. The individual in charge of the audit program should monitor progress in implementing remedial action.
5. The director is ultimately responsible for assuring that remedial actions are implemented.

F. **Managing the Quality Assurance Program**
   1. The director or senior clinician has ultimate responsibility for the quality assurance program and should be intimately involved in the review process on an ongoing basis.
   2. One should assign tasks to specific individuals and clearly define the roles of all personnel involved.
   3. Open communication and cooperation between management and providers is essential.
   4. One should use lay assessors for the abstraction of clinical records and for as many other routine tasks as possible.
   5. Organization systems must exist or be developed to allow one to conduct studies in an efficient and effective manner.
   6. It is the responsibility of the director to set deadlines and to assure that remedial actions are completed in a timely fashion.

### CLINICAL RECORDS REVIEW

1. The counselor will inform the administrative office when she or he needs a clinical record for review.
2. The designated office person will pull the record and place it in a separate box.
3. The record will be given to the provider so that he or she can verify that all the information needed is in the chart.
4. The counselor conducts the follow-up and review of the record.
5. The counselor then returns the clinical record to the administrative office for filing.

### CLINICAL RECORDS POLICY STATEMENT

A written client record must be maintained on every person who has been seen as a client. The client record is the who, what, why, where, when, and how of client care during a visit. For the record to be complete, it must contain sufficient information to identify the client, to justify the diagnosis and treatment, and to record the results of treatment.

The purposes of the client record are to:

1. Provide a means of communication between the provider and others condtributing to the client's care
2. Serve as a basis for planning individual client care
3. Furnish documentary evidence of the course of the client's condition and treatment during each visit
4. Serve as a basis for analysis, study, and evaluation of the quality of care rendered to the client
5. Assist in protecting the legal interests of the client, the pastoral counseling office, and the provider.
6. Provide clinical data for use in education or research

The methods of maintaining client records are:

1. Client records are maintained in accordance with the American Medical Record Association guidelines.
2. A family unit numbering system identifies each family. A family member numbering system identifies each client.
3. All records are filed in terminal digit using the family number, then by numerical order using the member number.
4. All client records are the property of the PCO.
5. The ICD-9-CM coding system is used to code diagnoses.
6. No client information is released without the consent of the client following state law governing the release of such information.
7. All client records must be returned to the proper storage facility within twenty-four hours of removal.
8. The attending counselor must review and initial all correspondence and reports before they are filed in the record.
9. The person making an entry must date and sign all record entries. The person signing should also give her or his professional status (e.g., Ph.D., Psy.D, M.S.W.).
10. Each client record that leaves the building for any reason is analyzed for accuracy before the record is refiled.
11. All client encounters are reviewed against the client records for completeness and accuracy.

## MAINTAINING CLIENT INDEX CARDS

1. One initiates an index card when a counselor first sees a client.
2. It contains the following:
   a. Client name
   b. Chart number
   c. Sex
   d. Birth date
   e. Telephone number
   f. Home address
3. Index cards should be a color selected by the person in charge and are filed in terminal digit order.
4. Index cards remain as a permanent record of all clients who have an established record.

## FAMILY INDEX CARDS

1. Family index cards are prepared on a daily basis.
2. The family index card contains the following:
   a. Name of head of household
   b. Name of client
   c. Address
   d. Telephone number
   e. Chart number
   f. Name of spouse or head of household
   g. Names of other family members
   h. Birth dates
   i. Payment history
   j. Date of registration
3. Family index cards are arranged in alphabetical order and remain as a permanent record of all clients who have been registered at the PCO.
4. An update of index cards is made when addresses change or members are added or deleted.

## RECORD RETRIEVAL

Receipt of a request for use of a client record activates the following procedures:
1. One looks for the record in the active patient file section according to the client number.
2. If the record is there, one replaces it with an out-guide and gives the record to the person requesting it.
3. If the record is not in the file and an out-guide has replaced it, one looks for the record at the location indicated on the out-guide. If the record is there, one puts the out-guide in the active section in its proper location.
4. If the record is not in the active file and no out-guide is replacing it, one looks for the record in the inactive section of the client file area.
5. If one locates the record in the inactive file area, one places an out-guide in the proper location in the active client file section.
6. If the record is not in the inactive section, one should check the card file to be sure a record has been made.
7. If no record has been made, one should check the information with the reception desk, then follow the procedure for establishing a new record.
8. If a record has been made, then one must look in all possible places for the record.
9. If the record still cannot be located, one must inform the attending counselor.
   Note: One must be diligent and continue looking for the chart during available time periods until it has been found.

## CLIENT RECORD RETRIEVAL FOR CLIENTS HAVING AN APPOINTMENT

1. With a yellow highlighter the appointment person marks the counselor's name on the appointment list.
2. The appointment person then pulls the record from the file, places the record on the table, and groups records according to counselor's name. Each removed record is replaced by an out-guide. The out-guide lists the date the record was removed and the name of the counselor.

3. When a record is not in the files and there is an out-guide, the appointment person writes the record's previous destination on the new request card.
4. When neither out-guide nor record is in the file, the appointment person writes "C.O." (complete out) on a new request card.
5. The appointment person maintains the out-guides of records that were C.O. in a separate file and later checks the client card file.
6. The appointment person places a red slash mark next to the client's name on the appointment list when the records have been located.
7. The appointment person checks each record to assure that each client has a signed consent form. If there is no consent form, one should place a blank consent form loose in the record to remind the provider that it must be signed by the client.
8. One should stamp the progress notes for the added appointments as follows:
   a. Client identification
   b. Date of appointment
   c. Counselor's name
   Then one places the record in the counselor's bin in terminal digit order.

## CLIENT RECORD ORGANIZATION

The client record is divided into two parts with dividers for each half. The left half is basically noncounseling information, except for an active problem list and flow sheets. The right half has all the counseling information. Each divider should have the following:

### Left Side

1. Problem list
   The problem list summarizes the problems identified during sessions that merit further follow-up. The problems are listed chronologically.
2. Correspondence
   In this specific order, starting from top to bottom, copies of:
   a. Records release forms
   b. Insurance or disability forms
   c. Letters mailed to patient
   d. School, work, or physical examination forms
   e. Treatment authorization form
   f. Miscellaneous information

### Right Side

In this specific order from top to bottom:
1. Record of counseling
   a. Progress notes
   b. Physical examination record
   c. History form
2. Referrals, reports (from top to bottom)
   a. Reports in chronological order:
      Counsultations
      Follow-up treatment
   b. Replies for requested record releases

## LOCATING LOST CLINICAL RECORDS

If one cannot locate a client record, one should search extensively until the record is found.

1. When a client record is not found, one should check the out-guide for the date of the request and the name of the requester. If a counselor saw the client the previous day, then one should check the following areas:
   a. The client records to be filed
   b. The billing area where client records are ready to be processed
   c. The counselor's office
2. If the record is not in those areas, one should check in all the other counseling rooms.
3. If the client record is still missing three business days after the search began, one should notify the director or senior counselor.
4. One must then reconstruct the client record.
   a. One should state on the client index card that the original record is missing and note the date the duplicate was started.
   b. One must prepare a new record folder and on the folder write, "Duplicate—Original Missing" and the date.
   c. One should request copies of relevant counseling information. After receiving the information, one should record "Duplicate—Original Missing" and the date.
   d. One should continue to search. If the original is found, one should destroy the duplicate.

## RELEASING INFORMATION OVER
## THE TELEPHONE

Telephone requests for client record information require proper identification and verification to assure that the requesting party is entitled to receive such information. One should maintain a record noting the request and the information released.
1. When someone outside the PCO calls and requests information over the phone, the staff member should ask the following:
   a. Client's name, birth date, and social security number
   b. Name of the caller
   c. Organization or location of the caller
   d. Telephone number of the caller
2. One should tell the caller that someone will return the call as soon as possible.
3. One should pull the client record and give it to the person in charge of releasing information.
4. The person in charge will return the call after ensuring that the requesting party is entitled to receive such information.

## RELEASE OF WRITTEN
## CLIENT RECORD INFORMATION

Here is an outline of the policy and procedures for the release of client record information.
1. The record pertaining to an individual client is the property of the PCO. The record shall be maintained to serve the client, the counselor, and the PCO in accordance with legal and regulatory agency requirements. The information con-

tained in the record belongs to the client, and the client is entitled to have the information protected from unauthorized release.

2. It shall be the general policy that the PCO will not voluntarily use the record in any manner that would jeopardize the interests of the client, with the exception that the PCO itself will use the record, if necesary, to defend itself or its agents.

3. Current users of information within the PCO and the purposes for which the information is used are classified as follows:

   a. Primary provider
      1) As a medium of communication among providers during the current phase of treatment
      2) As a reference for future treatment
      3) For training of other personnel and to assist students to relate theory with practice
      4) For prospective and retrospective evaluation of the quality of care through review and analysis of patterns of care as documented in the record
      5) For promotion of effective and efficient use of facilities, equipment, services, personnel, and financial resources through statistical analysis of information abstracted from the record
      6) For documentation of voluntary compliance with standards for accreditation of the institution or certification of an individual counselor
      7) For research aimed at the improvement of treatment or assessment of the effectiveness of other treatment through the study of appropriate cases
      8) For documentation that demonstrates conformity to government regulation
      9) For follow-up care of clients with long-term conditions and assessment of the efficiency of the care given

   b. Other center personnel
      The definition of center personnel includes psychiatrists, psychologists, counselors, and supporting clerical and technical persons. The center personnel will use the client records as needed to provide care.

   c. Administration
      1) Client information will be released only in connection with potential or actual litigation.
      2) In response to a complaint, the PCO's administrative authority decides whether to release necessary client information.

4. The PCO will release client information without a written authorization in the following instances:

   a. To health care providers: The PCO may disclose information to another health care facility or its professional staff to aid in the diagnosis or treatment of a patient.

   b. Billing: The PCO or other providers may disclose client information to a person or entity responsible for paying a client's bill, to the extent necessary to allow the payer to determine responsibility for payment and to make payment.

   c. Administrative billing services:
      1) One may disclose client information to any person or entity providing billing, claims management, data processing, or other administrative services on behalf of providers or third-party payers.
      2) Employees of the PCO are to be instructed in policies of confidentiality and are subject to penalties arising from violation as specified in these policies.

d. Peer review: Client information may be disclosed to professional certification or review authorities in order to aid them in reviewing the competence or qualifications of an individual practitioner.

e. Licensing or accreditation review: The PCO may permit persons who review licensing or accreditation to inspect information about clients, but they may not remove the information from the facility.

f. County coroner: One must disclose client information to the county coroner in the course of an investigation by the coroner's office.

g. Law enforcement agencies: Information may be disclosed to law enforcement agencies only with the written consent of the patient.

h. Public health department: One shall release only information pertaining to communicable disease.

i. Medical research: Information may be disclosed to research organizations or accredited educational institutions for purposes of bona fide research. The PCO will take reasonable steps to ensure that the research is legitimate and is attended by proper safeguards. This information is given without client's identification.

j. Disclosure to client's employer: Client information may be disclosed to the client's employer without the client's written authorization when the employer requested and paid for the counseling services. The information must be for use in proceedings in which the employer and the client are parties and in which the client has placed his or her clinical condition at issue; and the information must describe a condition that has an effect on the client's performance in the workplace.

k. Application for coverage or benefit: The PCO may release client information to a sponsor, insurer, or administrator of an insurance plan or policy from which the client seeks coverage or benefits if the information was created at the prior written request and expense of the requester for the specific purpose of evaluating the client's application for coverage or benefits.

l. Court orders: The PCO must release client information in response to a court order, which may be delivered in person or through the mail.

m. Administrative agency order: A board, commission, or administrative agency that is engaging in adjudication may issue an order for client information, if authorized by law. In that case, the PCO must release the information as if the order were from a court of law.

n. Subpoena: A party to a proceeding before a court or administrative agency may issue a subpoena, subpoena duces tecum, or notice to appear covering client information held by a provider. If one has a question about the validity of a particular subpoena, one should consult legal counsel.

o. Investigative subpoena: Boards, commissions, or administrative agencies may have authority to issue a subpoena in the course of an investigation.

p. Arbitration order: Either an arbitrator or an arbitration panel may issue an order authorizing the discovery of client information in an arbitration.

5. Data collection policy

a. All individuals engaged in the collection, handling, or dissemination of information will be specifically informed of their responsibility to protect client data and of the penalty of violation of this trust. Proven violation of confidentiality of client information will be cause for immediate termination of access to further data, and immediate termination of an employer-employee relationship with no consideration of reemployment. This policy will be made known to all employees at the time of employment and a signed acknowledgment form will be kept with each employee's personnel record.

b. The collection of any data relating to a client, whether by interview, observation, or review of documents, will be conducted in a setting that provides maximum security and protects the information from unauthorized individuals.

c. If the client wishes to correct data, it shall be done as an amendment, without change to the original entry, and shall be clearly identified as an additional document appended to the original client record at the direction of the client. This document shall then be regarded as an integral part of the client record.

6. Access to client records
   a. All requests for client records shall go to the office of the director.
   b. Release of information from the client record shall be carried out in accordance with all applicable legal, accreditation, and regulatory agency requirements.
   c. All authorized personnel shall have clinical records available for use within the facility for direct client care.
   d. Subject only to specific contraindications by the attending counselor and to any legal constraints such as those governing minors and those adjudicated as incompetent, a client or any representative designated by the client may have access to her or his own record for review upon written request with reasonable notice.
   e. All information contained in the client record is confidential and the release of information will be closely controlled. A properly completed and signed authorization is required for release of all health information except:
      1) As required by law
      2) For release to another provider currently involved in the evaluation or care of the client
      3) For medical care evaluation
      4) For research and education in accordance with conditions specified in policies
   f. A properly completed and signed authorization to release patient information shall include at least the following data:
      1) The name of the organization that is to release the information
      2) The name of the individual or institution that is to receive the information
      3) The client's full name and date of birth
      4) The purpose or need for the information
      5) The extent or nature of the information to be released, including dates of treatment
      6) The specific date, event, or condition upon which consent will expire unless revoked earlier
      7) A statement that a consent can be revoked but not retroactive to the release of information made in good faith prior to the revocation
      8) The date that consent is signed
         Note: The date of signature must be later than the date of information to be released
      9) The signature of the client or legal representative
         Note: In the case of treatment administered to a minor without parental knowledge, the PCO shall refrain from releasing the portion of the record relevant to this episode of care when responding to a request for information for which the signed authorization is that of the parent or guardian. An authorization by the minor shall be required in this instance.

g. All requests for information from client records shall go to the PCO director for authorization.

h. Information released to authorized individuals or agencies shall be strictly limited to information required to fulfill the purpose stated on the authorization. Release of information that is not essential to the stated purpose of the request is specifically prohibited.

i. After the authorized release of client information, the signed authorization will be retained in the record with a notation of the specific information released, the date of release, and the signature of the individual who released the information.

j. Client records shall be made available for research to individuals who have obtained approval for their research projects from the administrative or center director. Any research project that would involve the researcher contacting the client must have written permission of the client's attending counselor and the center director or a designee prior to contact.

k. The names, addresses, and dates of visits to a patient shall not be released to the news media or commercial organizations without the express written consent of the patient or the authorized agent of the patient.

7. Storage of clinical records

a. All clinical records shall be housed in physically secure areas under the immediate control of the person responsible for the clinical record area.

b. Client records shall be preserved safely for a minimum of seven years from the last visit, except that the record of unemancipated minors shall be kept at least seven years after such minor has reached the age of twenty-one years.

c. When in use within the PCO, client records must be kept in secure areas at all times. Client records should be available and accessible at all times for client care.

## RESPONDING TO CLIENT RECORD REQUESTS FROM OTHER HEALTH FACILITIES, PHYSICIANS, THIRD-PARTY PAYERS, ATTORNEYS, OR OUTSIDE AGENCIES

Upon receiving a request for client information, one must verify that the request meets the requirement of an authorization to release client information as specified in the policies of the PCO. The person receiving the request must:

1. Stamp the date that the request was received
2. Locate the client record number
3. Write the client record number on the request
4. Pull the client record from the file
5. Compare the client's signature on the request form against the consent or registration form in the client record
6. Photocopy only the requested information, which is usually progress notes, unless the request asks for more specific information
7. Also photocopy the request form and retain the copy as a permanent part of the record
8. Log the following information in a release of information log:
   a. The client record number
   b. The client's name
   c. The place to which information is being released

d. The information being sent
e. The date the information is sent

## RECOMMENDED POLICY STATEMENT GOVERNING SECURITY AND CONFIDENTIALITY OF CLIENT RECORDS

1. Client records are maintained in accordance with the American Medical Records Association guidelines.
2. A family unit numbering system identifies each family. A member numbering system identifies each patient.
3. All records are filed in terminal digit order using the family number, then the numerical order using the member number.
4. All client records are the property of the PCO.
5. The ICD-9-CM coding system is used to code diagnoses.
6. No client information is released without the consent of the patient following state law governing the release of such information.
7. All client records must be returned to their proper place of storage at the end of the day.
8. The attending counselor must initial all correspondence before it is filed in the client record.
9. Staple all copies together including the copy of the record request form
10. Mail copies to the address given in the record request

## RECOMMENDED CLIENT GRIEVANCE POLICY

A grievance system provides each client an opportunity to submit a complaint or concern for prompt consideration. It offers the client reasonable certainty that the problem will be aired and resolved. One should consider the grievance procedure as an administrative mechanism by which clients and the PCO may resolve their differences without resorting to external remedies such as litigation.

This grievance procedure provides an orderly fact-finding process to respond to client concerns. It is designed to provide a timely avenue of appeal for unresolved grievances that may involve a higher level of authority, but also makes every effort to allow for conflict resolution at the lowest possible level. In addition, the procedure provides a mechanism of tabulating data for periodic review by management to rectify problem areas within the system.

1. Person responsible
   a. Managing the grievance system is the responsibility of the senior counselor, who reports directly to the director. The function of the senior counselor is to receive grievances and complaints, to be responsible for the maintenance of grievance procedures, and to assist in the review of emergent patterns for the formulation of policy changes and procedural improvements.
   b. The senior counselor is the point of first contact for filing a grievance.
2. Form for submitting grievance
   Each complaint received in person, by telephone, or by written communication shall be recorded on a grievance record form. The recorded information shall include:
   a. Serial number of grievance form

    b. Date the form is being filled out
    c. Name of client
    d. Address of client
    e. Telephone number of client
    f. Person filing complaint and phone number
    g. Relationship to client
    h. Location of provider
    i. Dates of problem
    j. Was service received
    k. Description of complaint
    l. Resolution
    m. Signature of senior counselor and date
    n. Date of administration follow-up (if required)
    o. Date of referral to rights committee (if required)

3. Follow-up action taken (time period) log, files
    a. The senior counselor will attempt to resolve each grievance immediately. All grievances not resolved within a specified time period may require the gathering of more detailed information.
    b. The senior counselor shall maintain a log of actions taken.

4. Client rights committee
    a. The client rights committee shall act upon the facts of each case. Members of this committee shall be present at all requested hearings.
    b. Recommended actions of the client rights committee shall be submitted to the director for confirmation, revision, or denial.

# APPENDIX 5

# SUGGESTED POLICY STATEMENTS

The board of directors of PCOs should adopt policies to address a variety of situations that confront counselors: how to handle suicidal or violent persons, when to make referrals, and when to report to authorities. These policies need to be periodically reviewed for changes in local and state law. They should be developed with the advice of legal counsel to assure that the policies are consistent with the law and do address the reasonably expected problems that counselors will face. Having such policies assures that management seeks to have a consistent, uniform approach to problems, giving helpful guidance to individual counselors whose clients are in crisis. Such policies, first developed and stated, can then be refined as experience dictates. To assist PCOs in drafting policy statements, the following problems and suggested policies are proposed as starting points:

## SUICIDAL IDEATION

*Scenario #1:* B tells counselor that he has been thinking of killing himself and has actually planned how to do it. He has the means and the intent. What should the counselor do?

**Suggested policy**

If a counselee appears to have the means and intent to commit suicide, the counselor must stay with the counselee, secure additional emergency assistance from other staff and local officials or police, and follow the case through to voluntary/involuntary commitment.

*Scenario #2:* C tells counselor that she doesn't think her life is worth living. Her mental state and emotional affectation are generally depressed, her consideration appears unfocused and nonspecific. The counselor makes a judgment call that she is not in immediate danger but should see a medical doctor. What next should the counselor do?

**Suggested policy**

If a counselee manifests nonspecific suicidal ideation but does not appear to be in immediate danger of harm, a referral to a physician is indicated. Depending on the degree of concern appropriate to the situation, the counselor should follow the case to the point of being reassured that the case is being followed by medical personnel. Note: if there is a prior history of suicidal attempts, then treat the counselee as an immediate threat case (see policy to scenario #1).

*Scenario #3:* D tells counselor with some emotion that her husband has recently threatened to kill himself and she fears that he will carry out the threat. Should the counselor intervene?

**Suggested policy**

If a counselee reports that a family member has threatened harm to himself, the family member should be assisted in making a report to the authorities.

## THREATENED HARM TO OTHERS

*Scenario #4:* E asks the counselor not to tell anybody, but he has abused his child repeatedly and needs help. Can the counselor keep the confidence? Is there a duty to report?

**Suggested Policy**
All counselees sign an intake form waiving confidentiality and privacy rights when disclosure by a counselor is required by law. The counselor does not then keep the confidence, but reports in accordance with state law the alleged abuse, which is reasonably suspected based upon the counselee's disclosure.

*Scenario #5:* F admits that she is stealing drugs from her employer, a pharmacy, to support her drug habit. She will not or cannot stop. Should the counselor report this?

**Suggested Policy**
The counselor will help counselees become accountable for their illegal acts by providing them an opportunity to self-report before filing a report with the authorities. If the action is past and not continuing, and restitution is appropriate, the counselor will seek to monitor progress in repairing relationships.

*Scenario #6* G is angry and tells his counselor that he has a gun and will shoot Y. He has a motive. His counselor believes he could act on his threat. Should the counselor warn Y?

**Suggested Policy**
Counselors will warn intended victims of real threats made in their presence. Threats not made in their presence require a judgment call as it may be more difficult to assess how realistic the threat is. If the threat is made by someone with a violent history, the threat should be reported to the police.

## NOTIFICATION

The foregoing situations raise the question of under what circumstances employees are required to notify management or supervisors when problems arise. Other situations that trigger the policy requiring notification might be when a counselor's caseload exceeds a maximum number of hours per week; when counseling is given to persons who have not completed an intake form, and are therefore not registered with the PCO; or when a counselor has knowledge of a threat or actual legal claim against the PCO or the counselor. Policies can be developed for each of these situations to fit the need of the PCO.

## REFERRALS

Since counselors who work in a PCO make referrals to health care providers, a policy can establish that they will make referrals to those on a preapproved list, to persons of known reputation, qualification, and experience.

## CONFLICT OF INTEREST

Care should be given to the development of policies that will assure avoidance of dual representation, counseling of family members, management of transference and counter transference phenomena, simultaneous provision of mental health care services by a mental health professional.

## ASSIGNMENT POLICY

Management has an interest in assuring that the most difficult problems presented are matched with expertise within the PCO. It should not be presumed that all counselees can be treated by any counselor or that all counselors are equally qualified. Having counselors on staff who have developed an expertise by experience or training will carry a legal presumption that management will match need with expertise. If counselors are not assigned to counsel clients based upon any particular criteria of qualifications/expertise, it is important to have a policy of review after the initial intake form is completed in order to confirm that the counselor is appropriate to the case. Such a policy will develop criteria by which a reassignment would be made if necessary.

# BIBLIOGRAPHY

Bednar, R. L., S. C. Bednar, M. J. Lambert, and D. R. Waite. 1981. *Psychotherapy with High-Risk Clients: Legal and Professional Standards*. Pacific Grove, Calif.: Brooks/Cole Publishing Company.

*Best's Review*. 1991. Editorial. (May).

Bush, J. C., and W. H. Tiemann. 1989. *The Right to Silence: Privileged Communication and the Law*, 3rd ed. Nashville: Abingdon Press.

Dankmyer, T., and J. Grow. 1977. Taking steps for safety's sake. *Hospitals* (May 16): 51, 62.

Edelwich, J., and A. Brodsky. 1991. *The Sexual Dilemmas for the Helping Professional*. New York: Brunner/Mazel.

Gallegher, R. B. 1956. Risk management: New phase of cost control. *Harvard Business Review* (September-October) 34:5.

George, J. M. 1970. When is a hospital liable for negligence to its patients? *Canadian Hospital* (October) 47: 26-27.

Group for the Advancement of Psychiatry. 1991. *The Mental Health Professional and the Legal System*. New York: Brunner/Mazel.

Haas, L. J., and J. L. Malouf. 1989. *Keeping Up the Good Work: A Practitioner's Guide to Mental Health Ethics*. Sarasota, Fla.: Professional Resource Exchange, Inc.

Hedrick, William. 1992. Personal communication. Fort Lauderdale, Fla.

Liberman, A. 1988. *A Risk & Insurance Management Guide for Medical Group Organizations*. Denver: Center for Research in Ambulatory Health Care Administration Press.

Mehr, R. I., and B. A. Hedges. 1963. *Risk Management in the Business Enterprise*. Homewood, Ill: Richard D. Irving, Inc., 89.

Negley, Edward T. 1983. Personal communication. Cedar Grove, N.J.

Peterson, M. R. 1992. *At Personal Risk: Boundary Violations in Professional-Client Relationships*. New York: Norton.

Rankin, W. W. 1990. *Confidentiality and Clergy: Churches, Ethics, and the Law*. Harrisburg: Morehouse Publishing.

Senge, P. M. 1990. *The Fifth Discipline: The Art and Practice of the Learning Organization*. New York: Doubleday.

Simon, R. I. 1987. *Clinical Psychiatry and the Law*. Washington, D.C.: American Psychiatric Press, Inc.

Vaughan, E. J. 1986. *Fundamentals of Risk and Insurance Management*. New York: John Wiley and Sons, 3.

Wood, J. C. 1975. Risk management. *Risk and Health Care Financing* (Summer) 1:56.

Woody, R. H. 1988. *Fifty Ways to Avoid Malpractice: A Guidebook for Mental Health Professionals*. Sarasota, Fla.: Professional Resource Exchange, Inc.